Praise for *From Frazzled . . . ...astic!*

"I picked up *From Frazzled to Fantastic* with the intention of flipping through it. Two hours later I'd read it cover to cover. I will read it again and again—next time slower, to savor. Lynn Durham is a gifted teacher, writer, and philosopher. She combines wit, charm, and the wisdom of Yoda, moving you from ha-ha to a-ha at the speed of laughter. Heart touching, entertaining, and powerfully effective: You're just one thought away from entertainment and inspiration."

-Karyn Buxman, RN, MSN, CSP, CPAE
Publisher, Journal of Nursing Jocularity

"Lynn has written a power packed manual for living un-encumbered by anxiety, doubt and the million negative thoughts that hold us captive. Read just a page or many pages and unlock the truth of who you truly are. I have often preached the "power of now" and in *From Frazzled to Fantastic* Lynn reveals practical advice on how to stay present. She and what she has written are a blessing."

-Ronald Piro, Retired General Manager
CBS Radio and Nassau Broadcasting

"This beautiful book contains page after page of uplifting thoughts and suggestions to make your day more positive, productive and fruitful! Lynn's emphasis on shifting your focus and giving thanks will set you on a new path for your life. Her personal experiences bring authenticity and light to this gem of a book!"

-Dolores Wilkie, Sykesville, MD

"I usually loathe cheery little self-help books and groaned to myself when I saw how it started, but it captivated me in spite

i

of myself. Refreshingly free of the usual platitudes, or when there are any, they are expressed freshly with a nice twist. Glad I took the time for it today."
-Wendie Howland, RN, MN, CRRN, CCM, CNLCP
Editor, AANLCP Journal of Nurse Life Care Planning

"Self-help books have been top sellers as people seek ways to feel better and become more "stress-hardy" as Lynn describes it. This book is for those people! The content is joyful and sensitive yet practical and powerful. I can just imagine the positive outcomes readers will have as a result of experiencing and integrating this goldmine of inspiration."
-Brian Jud, Host of the TV show
"The Book Authority"

"I read this beautiful book on an airplane and could not put it down. The wisdom, the practical advice, and the deep love Lynn brings to us are a welcome and refreshing tonic for the negativity, fear, and hopelessness in today's world. Thank you, Lynn, for reminding us of God's grace, our own choices, and the many blessings of this precious life."
-Barbara Glanz, Speaker and author of 9 books
including CARE Packages for the Workplace

"Feeling stressed? A tad frazzled? Want a solution? It's in your hands... Lynn Durham's *From Frazzled to Fantastic* will soothe your soul and celebrate your successes. Woven with wonderful humor and ahas ... this is just what the savvy doctor would order!"
-Dr. Judith Briles, The Book Shepherd, author of 28
books including Show Me About Book Publishing

"These pages hold the secret for transforming your mind and your heart - taking you to fresh realms of daily joy!"
-Glenna Salsbury, CSP, CPAE Speaker Hall of Fame,
author of The Art of the Fresh Start

"We all have days when things "should be" better or days when we are exhausted and the end doesn't seem to be in sight. Pick up this book! You will probably see yourself here and you will learn how to change your thoughts to get the kind of positive results you want."
- Ivan Burnell, author of *The Power of Positive Doing,*
and Living in an Unlimited Universe

"How can anyone not leap into a book called *'From Frazzled to Fantastic!'* -- it's for everyone who's ready to dive into vibrant living. It's literally like singing from the inside out!"
-Soleira Green author of The Alchemical Coach
Co-Founder of the Visionary Network

"Yes, Lynn is right. Thoughts are things. THOUGHTS ARE EVERYTHING. Open up Lynn's book to any chapter and you'll be reading just what you need to change your life for the better. Then pass on these life lessons to everyone you know."
-Joe Sabah, Author of How to Get on Radio Talk Shows
All Across America Without Leaving Your Home or Office

Lynn Durham

FROM FRAZZLED

TO FANTASTIC!

YOU'RE ONE THOUGHT AWAY
FROM FEELING BETTER

Lynn Durham, RN, BSN

Squam Lakes Publishing

Also by Lynn Durham
Dancing Gracefully With Life

Note to Reader:
No book can replace the services of a qualified mental health specialist. This book is solely for information and enjoyment. If you are having problems please seek medical care.

FROM FRAZZLED TO FANTASTIC – YOU'RE ONE THOUGHT AWAY FROM FEELING BETTER.

Copyright ©2012 by Lynn Durham.

ISBN-13: 978-1467978644
ISBN-10: 1467978647

For information, address Squam Lakes Publishing
PO Box 536, Holderness, NH 03245
www.squamlakespublishing.com

Cover photo: Patricia Werner Bender
Author photo: Robert Snelling

Printed in the United States of America.

CONTENTS

ACKNOWLEDGMENTS

THANK YOU!!

Some people here are dear friends, some people intersected my life at an important point. Some are living now and some living on in my memory. I count you all among my Blessings.

To my Mom and Dad, Irene and John, Brett, Tyler and Joshua, Kerstin, Devin and Beth, Sue and Amiee, Alyssa and Heidi, what a wonderful family!

Thank you to Norma Adams, Liz Ashe, Peg Baim, Pat Bender, Mary Hillyer Blackmar, Judith Briles, Les Brown, Nancy Burke, Christine Bushway, Bill Coombs, Ken Hamilton, Sheila Davis, Ed Dixon, Jayne Lloyd, George Engdahl, Judy Fabian, Valla Dana Treuman, Barbara Glanz, Joel Goodman and Margie Ingram, John Haywood, Anne Helmke, Sam Horn, Brian Jud, Dick Kane, Cathy King, Rita LaBruzzo, Laurel Lent, Carolyn Long, David Lundblad, Pat and Warren Mackensen, Al Casassa, Elaine Magillicuddy, Bill and Pauline Maloney, Pam McPhee, Jane Milotte, Cathy Corbett McKinnon, Nan McQuade, Rosita Perez, John Haywood, Karen Reid, Roger and Gwen Rice, Father Bob Sandoz, Patt Schwab, Kathy Stilwell, Mark and Tina Walker, Sister Kathleen Walsh, The Webbers, Dolores and Steve Wilkie, Ivan and Dagney Burnell, Sheryl Wookey, Charles Cudjoe, Rick LeBro, Holly

Elkins, Kevin Stacey, Alan Weiss, Laura and Tom Lagana, Tom McMullen, Conor O'Reily, Kathleen Hassan, Wendie Howland, Doug Germann, and Mary Busha.

I appreciate those who I didn't know well but who reached out and offered words of encouragement along my way.

My gratitude to those who read these words and gave me feedback in the process.

Thanks to my coaching and speaking clients, retreat participants, students, audiences, readers, friends and those authors whose words enriched me.

And thank you God!

I am so richly blessed by these encounters.

FOREWORD

Fate (what I now call SerenDestiny) brought Lynn and me together years ago at Joel Goodman's Humor Conference in Saratoga Springs where I was the keynote speaker. I delighted in her enthusiasm for life - which is evident in this book as you keep turning the pages to see what's next.

The snippets of stories make this an easy read and her unique perspective is engaging. This book is like a buffet for people hungry for heartfelt insights. Lynn not only shares recent medical research, she gives innovative suggestions to help us create our own good thoughts, ones that will change our body chemistry and allow us to look and feel wonderful instead of worse!

"Vigor is contagious," noted Ralph Waldo Emerson, "and whatever makes us either think or feel more strongly adds to our power."

From Frazzled to Fantastic provides insights that have the power to increase your vigor and help you feel better and stronger. This will give you added energy that allows you to elevate those around you.

Read it and reap.

Sam Horn, The Intrigue Expert,
author of *POP!* and the upcoming
SerenDestiny and *Eyebrow Test*

PREFACE

Life has not ceased to amaze me. At every age I have found beauty and gifts that I never would have imagined. Life is wonder-full, and when we can look through wonder-filled eyes, the beauty and the blessings come into focus and we reap the physical and emotional benefits that follow that new vision. It is we who decide whether we feel wonderful or worse by the thoughts we hold.

I never considered myself a writer; my sister was the English major and teacher. I'm a nurse. Science and math were my forte, so I was surprised when after writing a letter to the editor of a statewide New Hampshire paper he called and invited me to write a monthly column.

The column was well-received. Any concern I had about finding new material vanished as the more I wrote, the more I became aware of new stories. I've had monthly columns for years, locally, statewide and nationally. The subject matter of the columns and word counts differ. While some are more academic, my favorites are those offering images of moments in time that can be translated or expanded into larger lessons. These snapshots of life, and my view of seeing what we find there, have attracted a faithful following, and I am told, "Go a long way to give people peace."

This book is similar to my favorite columns, filled with different snippets about life. There are stories, comments, suggestions, quotes and references to medical research rich in proving the psychological and physical benefits in healthy thinking and feeling good.

Look over the "new thoughts" at the end of each segment with an open mind and see if there are any you can use that would help you see life in other ways, ways that will you bring peace.

Lynn Durham

We don't need more money, we don't need greater
success or fame, we don't need the perfect body or even
the perfect mate. Right now, at this very moment, we
have a mind, which is all the basic equipment we need to
achieve complete happiness. Dalai Lama

FIRST THOUGHTS

You're one thought away from feeling better.

I guess anyone who picks up this book wants to feel better. No, that may not be true. Maybe they want to see what someone says about feeling better because it seems that there are some people who are happy with their misery.

I asked someone if he wanted to feel better and he said, "I don't know." For some people unhappiness serves a purpose somehow. Have they been rewarded in this behavior in some way? Do they like that others feel sorry for them? Do they benefit from more attention? How about you?

You may be willing to wish for your happiness but are you willing to do the work to achieve it? Are you willing to change your mind about some things? Or do you get too much benefit out of whining and complaining?

This is for the people out there like one woman who told me, "I didn't know happiness was my choice."

Even if there has been a perceived "kind of reward" to your unhappiness, I'll show you it's not worth it. Besides, you are probably the person who does want to feel better. And for you, I will give you tips and techniques to increase your sense of well-being and help you move from frazzled to fantastic.

1

Because: "You are one thought away from feeling better, and you can quote your Well Being Coach on that one!"

What I present here is a smorgasbord of tips. When I give my programs I may tell people to be still and we do a guided visualization or maybe get people up and dancing. The truth is there are so many possibilities and only you know what you need at any given moment. My suggestion is you check in with yourself. Just as different people need different things so too an individual may have different needs at different times. You are on a journey of discovery to find out new ways of looking, thinking and feeling about life. Then you can decide what serves you best – one thought at a time.

As in any life, mine has had times that didn't seem so good. Yet when I get far enough away from those circumstances, I can look back and find benefits. Sometimes I am even wise enough to see some "gifts" while still in the midst of an experience that others might label "bad."

I've noticed that when I become aware of my thoughts and when it's necessary change them, I feel better. As a nurse, I know our thoughts can trigger the release of stress hormones that can start a cascade of other changes in the body, including changing the heart variability pattern, reducing immune function, creating less happiness, aging more rapidly, shortening lifespans, and causing a number of other physical and mental problems.

For these reasons, I invite you on this journey of observation. Consider your thinking and focus on the thoughts that bring you more peace, are more loving or bring you more joy.

When I was young, I remember my mother talking about how difficult it was for her to see when she was driving at night, especially in the rain. I couldn't understand it because I could see just fine. Recently I noticed that I, too, was having more difficulty seeing at night to drive, especially if it was raining. I started to understand what my mother was feeling in her inability to see clearly and I began to have more empathy for her predicament.

Then I had a wonderful awakening, a chance for better vision. If we look at things in a new way, we may be able to gain this clarity at any time. My oldest son Brett borrowed my car. When he came in he said, "Mom, you need a new windshield. The one you have is so pitted; it's hard to see through it."

Interesting, isn't it? We get so close to things that we don't notice the small changes. The windshield had traveled many miles with that car and with me. The sand and rocks that hit the glass made minor damage that was imperceptible at first, but worsened over time.

How many things in our lives are there that change so little at a time that we don't notice them at first? But when seen from a fresh perspective, with new eyes, we can perceive what the problem really is.

I replaced that windshield and was surprised to see how my vision was restored for driving at night, dry or wet roads. It made me wonder what other things in my life had become clouded and could become clearer by changing the lens through which I viewed them. Try asking yourself, "Could this event be better served with that optimistic, solution-oriented attitude, a faith-filled trust?" If so, then rose colored glasses might best serve you.

Some circumstances might call for "nose-covered" glasses, the ones with the attached mustache. You could use them to seek out the humor and joy in the situation. Looking back, situations that didn't seem so funny at the time can gain humor and grace in the retelling. If you think a circumstance

3

will be funny later, go ahead, think it's funny now. What in your life could you look at right now with more humor?

I think answering even one of those questions with an affirmative action would change what you see in your world. What will you do to restore your vision?

By the way, I wonder if my mother's problem had anything to do with an old windshield?

I want you to know that I realize that I'm not perfect at this. I can remember a time when I cried and thought, "I'm a fraud. I tell people that they're one thought away from feeling better, and here I am saying such terrible things to myself and feeling worse."

Then my sister pointed out to me, "Maybe you're 6 or 12 thoughts away!" That made me smile. It reminded me that possibly I just hadn't found the right thought ... yet.

I've gathered a collection of thoughts in this book so you can see which ones will resonate with you and meet your needs. If you have other thoughts that work well for you, please let me know smile@lynndurham.com

Use this book, turn pages, underline, write in the margins - interact, grow and change. This book will be short, and to the point on how you can change your life, one thought at a time.

 HERE'S ONE THOUGHT: How can I see this in another way, one that would bring me peace or joy?

GLAD GAME – THINKING THANKS

*Let us rise up and be thankful, for if we didn't learn a lot
today, at least we learned a little, and if we didn't learn
a little, at least we didn't get sick, and if we got sick,
at least we didn't die; so, let us all be thankful.*

Buddha

I think the Glad Game is a bright idea.

When I have been accused of such things as being a Pollyanna, I say, "Thank you!" Do you recall that movie and how a child changed the entire town?

In the beginning Pollyanna is with her father who is a missionary. They are opening a package and Pollyanna is hoping she'll be receiving a doll as she had requested. What they discover is a pair of crutches. Her dad gets her to play the Glad Game with him. "What could we be glad about?" They come up with the idea that they're glad because they don't need crutches.

After Pollyanna is orphaned, she goes to live with her stern aunt, and the little girl's infectious optimism is sprinkled about the town as she helps others to see what they might be glad about. Pollyanna ends up changing the entire town. What a powerful force for good she was. One person can make a great difference in the lives of many. In fact, you have no idea of where "what *you* do" may go.

Optimistic attitudes relate to your personal well-being. Medical research shows that optimists are healthier physically and psychologically.

In studies done with students, those who were optimistic were less likely to get sick prior to finals. In one research project, the only variable that emerged as a strong association to health was the belief that "life is positive and things will generally work out well in the end." Another finding showed fewer physical symptoms corresponded with these top three coping measures: problem-solving, planning and optimism. Studies of heart by-pass surgery patients revealed that optimists recovered faster. They were reported as being happier; and their lives normalized sooner.

Optimists take action, problem-solve, and plan for ways to deal with what they encounter. They are more accepting of their stressors, positively interpret, intend to grow from, and find meaning in them. The direct effect that optimism had on them was independent of any other variable.

A study of successful female executives showed humor and optimism moderated the ill effects of perfectionism on daily hassles and burnout. And in a study of women following breast surgery, optimistic women had less distress at each point in their treatment. There is good reference material on the University of Pennsylvania Positive Psychology Center site.

On the other hand, pessimism correlates with greater illness, passive responses and more negative life events. That's *following* the pessimistic attitude, not because of the events. So it's up to you.

The HeartMath Institute in Boulder Creek, California has demonstrated with the Heart Rate Variability Pattern how our attitudes can influence cardiac changes. When the subjects were feeling frustrated or angry there were random, jerky patterns. The good news is that by changing the thoughts and feelings to appreciation, this pattern shifts into a more coherent rhythm.

What do you want in your life? Do you want more health, faster recovery, psychological well-being, more adaptive skills, less distress? Then you want to choose the right thoughts.

 HERE'S ONE THOUGHT: What can I be "Glad" about here?

A wise man does not grieve for the things which he has not, but rejoices for those which he has. *Epictetus*

NEED A GRATTITUDE ADJUSTMENT?

My brother-in-law's mom's cottage was partially destroyed in a coastal storm. My mother was talking about how upsetting that was. On the other hand, my sister has the attitude that she wouldn't cry over anything that wouldn't cry about her. It sounded like a wise choice to me. Same circumstance, two thoughts.

You see the differences in people following disasters. Flood, fire, tornado, it doesn't matter. Reporters will talk with one "victim" who lost her home and all her belongings. This person is devastated. She looked and sounded like she'd never be able to be happy again.

Then the reporter shifts to another woman who says, "Thank goodness, none of us was hurt. It was so great the way the community pulled together. I can't believe the kindnesses offered to me by perfect strangers." (Is that why they call them perfect?)

The second "victim's" home was also destroyed and she lost all her belongings as well. Yet she chose a "victor" mentality. She counted their blessings.

At any point in your life, you have a choice. You can choose to think about what you have lost and whine ...or... you can focus on what you have left with gratitude. Which do you usually do?

In Apollo 13, Tom Hanks describes a time when he was flying, fuel was low and he couldn't locate the aircraft carrier. Then to make matters worse (he thought) the cabin lights went out. Now looking back from a new perspective, he sees that the failure of the lights was a gift. Because there were no lights in the plane, he saw the faint lights from the stirred up plankton following the ship and it guided him safely "home."

Many times if we wait, not judge, when we get farther down the road and look back we will see how things are working for good.

I encourage you to look for the goods and greats in your life. You're constantly "marinating" your mind. Is it in the misery or the mystery? Do you focus on what you wish were different, or do you focus on the things for which you are grateful? It's your choice!

 HERE'S ONE THOUGHT: I choose to "Think Thanks," there's a gift here somewhere; if I can't see it now, I'll notice it later.

9

The gem cannot be polished without friction, nor man perfected without trial. *Confucius*

ROCKING

You could think of yourself as a miner. Mining all starts with a dream, a hope, and a vision of discovering some of God's splendor. By looking, studying the landscape, researching information and watching for signs, you're more likely to succeed in your quest of finding the mother lode.

Or what if you thought of yourself as the rock? Do you feel pressured at times? The most valuable minerals are those that have been "pressed" into beauty. The great pressure of the earth has formed these magnificent specimens. What if those things that are squeezing you are causing you to become something more beautiful?

Prospecting. Are you ready, prepared, equipped? Sometimes it's "ready or not, here I come." Excavating, drilling, blasting, tunneling are some of the means of finding the gems. Yikes! Jack hammering, digging, cutting the extraneous away to get to the jewels that are hidden there just waiting to be released. Is there a rock hammer chipping away to remove what really isn't you? Do you know who you are at the core?

Maybe it's just a sifting process requiring patience, perseverance, working and waiting. Are you willing to labor? Do you have the stamina and endurance to do what needs to be done to find the richness of your life?

Do you realize you have to look carefully? You may need to learn to know what you're looking for. If you don't, you may throw away a valuable stone. Sometimes things of value are not recognized until they're polished. We need to know what to look for in ourselves and to look carefully in others as well. Because in judging by a surface glance we may be passing up the greatest treasure of all.

Finally found! There's the wonderful thrill of success of the search. Will you allow your Self to "get found"?

Uh, oh, still not finished. Now there's the grinding down, cutting and polishing. Why is it we think we'll be beautiful without shaping? Remember that the time and effort of the cutting and polishing is saved only for the most valuable of minerals. That would mean if you're feeling the friction, it's because you're worth it!

The many facets of the gems mirror the facets of who we are, who those around us are, and they mirror our lives. There are so many different aspects of each of us that we can know someone for years, and with the next conversation find out something about them we never knew before. We are all varied and diverse. Even more amazing is that there are so many distinct facets of ourselves of which we are unaware.

But life invites us to know.

When you search out where your heart's desires lead you, how your joy is found, and what your talents are, and then you go there, you can find a goldmine of success.

When you're willing to look below the surface for the beauty in others and yourself, you will unearth jewels.

When you embrace the challenges life has given you, and the friction causes you to become real, being fully who you are, your magnificence is magnified.

Get prospecting!

And be willing to answer life's invitation to "get found."

11

HERE'S ONE THOUGHT: With pressure like this, I'm sure I'm a diamond!

The greatest thing is to give thanks for everything. He who has learned this knows what it means to live. He has penetrated the whole mystery of life: giving thanks for everything. Albert Schweitzer

A BLESSINGOMETER

We measure all sorts of things. We have a pedometer to take on our walks and odometers even for our bicycles. We check the thermometer in the morning. I have a suggestion for another meter to check often. It's a blessingometer.

Have you seen those small hand-held tally counters? Each time you press the button it goes up one number. I recommend that you use one to count your blessings. Get one, keep it handy and click it each time you think of something for which you are grateful.

Check it each evening and note the number. Is it low? Is it increasing each day? What does it tell you? As you start to measure and note the gifts in your life, your focus will change and you'll start to see even more blessings. As you look deeper into each situation with the intention of finding something good in every circumstance, you *will* find it, and that awareness will release a special magic in your life.

I had roof ridge vents installed on my house to help it breathe better. Those who were reading my columns were probably thinking: "It's about time, someone who talks about the importance of breathing didn't have a house that could breathe?" What I noticed was, when I drove down the street, I

13

saw how many other houses had roof ridge vents. Before mine were installed, I hadn't been aware of them.

Just because I hadn't seen them didn't mean they weren't there. They've been there all along. I just didn't notice them. I believe it's the same in our lives. The blessings are there. If you don't see them, it's only because you haven't noticed or aren't looking for them. You can shift your focus. Are you willing to feel better?

If I asked you what was wrong in your life, would you list pages of problems without batting an eye? Could you name as many benefits? There is such poverty in the world. Places where they wash in rivers and spread clothes to dry in the grass. There are hospitals where equipment is lacking, where patients have to lie on the floors or on stretchers with no mattresses. In our country we have so much to be grateful for. Have you given thanks for the hospitals, medical equipment and professionals lately?

When I was working at a Visiting Nurse Association, I heard a grandmother excited about hearing the "tinkle" in the toilet when her grandson was in the bathroom. To parents, that noise can be music to the ears. And to this woman it was even more important. Her grandson had been unable to perform that function normally since birth. This was a new ability following surgery. How many times have you been thankful for all of the processes that are taking place in your body?

Our body is miraculous and constantly performing all kinds of chemical, physiological and life-supporting processes. If we cut ourselves a miracle of healing begins. Without any conscious help on our part our body starts healing that wound. Are you grateful for your ability to heal?

Our appreciation for the gifts in life is food for our spirits. When we open our eyes to our blessings, we feel nourished. Gratitude...it's just a selfish thing to do! Buy a blessingometer, use it, and tell me how it works in your life.

 HERE'S ONE THOUGHT: What am I taking for granted that someone else would cherish?

15

A hundred times a day I remind myself that my inner and outer life depends on the labors of other men, living and dead, and that I must exert myself in order to give in the measure as I have received and am still receiving.
Albert Einstein

DO IT WITH JOY

It is good to get clear on the fact that whatever you do, you are choosing to do it. Some may say, "No, I'm not," but the truth is, you are. You are deciding to do it over something else at each moment.

I was talking to my neighbor who was pregnant at the time. She complained because she was being "forced" to give up salt. I told her she was choosing to give up salt. She said she was not. She told me the doctor was "making" her do it. I again repeated she was choosing to do it. Again, she denied it was her choice. I told her, yes, it was. She could take salt. There it was, right in front of her on the table. "I can't take it. It would be bad for the baby," she said. Yes! She was choosing not to use the salt for her baby's well-being. It was indeed her choice, and it was a good one.

You are doing what you do anyway. You can choose to do it and be miserable, OR you can choose to do it and be happy. I recommend doing what you choose to do with joy. To live being joyful is a gift not only to yourself, but to all those around you.

Consider dishes or some other household task. You are choosing to do it or you wouldn't be doing it. Again, I can hear people saying, "No, I'm not." "Yes, you are." You may be choosing it because not choosing it would leave no dishes to use. Maybe you would rather have someone else do it, but now, you are doing it. You have somehow determined it was better than whatever the alternative was. The choice has been made or the water wouldn't be running. Realize it is your choice and do it with joy. This joy is not in reference to the dishwashing detergent!

You don't have to believe me on any of this. Do an experiment. Test it out and report back to me on what it was like. Acknowledge that you are indeed choosing to do this action over anything else at this time. It is a fact.

Now, since you are not getting out of it, really get into it. Be totally mindful of the experience. Feel the water temperature on your hands. Be in this moment fully. Are you thankful that you have running water, cold and hot? What about your hands. Think of all the things they've done for you. I broke my arm and I can tell you how fortunate you are if they work for you. Bless them.

Have you noticed all the soap bubbles and the rainbow of colors shimmering in them? Are you grateful for your eyes and the ability to see them?

Did you pay attention to the scent of the dishwashing liquid, to the sound of the water running or splashing? And were you grateful for your ability to smell and to hear?

Feel the smooth texture of the plates and think of the food they held and all that happened to bring it to your table, from your car and the grocery store, building and people. Think of the truckers, packing plants and employees. Go all the way back to the farmers and rain and earth and sun. Think of

17

the people who were sustained by that food. No doubt they were individuals you love. Consider all the benefits you can imagine, and rest in thankfulness.

For those who are willing to attempt this practice, you will find a different experience. This is mindfulness, constant prayer. The next time you wash your floor, think of the shelter this place has provided for you, the people you love who have walked here. Be thankful for your many blessings. Remember it will change the chemicals in your body, boost your immune system, alter your heart variability pattern and lower your blood pressure.

Whatever you do in this life, you can do it with anger and resentment (and create a caustic chemical stew in your body) OR you can do it with prayer and thanksgiving. How do you choose to live?

 HERE'S ONE THOUGHT: I am choosing to do this in this moment and I choose to do it with JOY.

EMBRACING WHAT IZ

*God, give us Grace to accept with serenity
the things that cannot be changed,
Courage to change the things
which should be changed,
and the Wisdom to distinguish
the one from the other.*
Reinold Niebuhr

I do keynotes, seminars and retreats focused on Mind Body Spirit wellness. In some of my programs I put on a pointed hat decorated with stars and moons and talk about the importance of being the *Wizard of What Iz*. It's amazing how long we will deny the truth and wish for what cannot be. I love Byron Katie's words: "When you argue with reality, you lose. But ....only 100 percent of the time."

As much as you might like things to be different, they are what they are. Not until you accept life just as you find it, do you do what's necessary. Burying your head under the covers doesn't work for long. You have to get up and get on with life sometime; you may as well start now.

When I was going through my divorce the words "Oh, Well!" worked in any number of circumstances and with a variety of inflections. You'll hear teenagers using the word "Whatever." We can too!

Just pick some thoughts, words or sayings that work for you.

 HERE'S ONE THOUGHT: I'll just add this to my "whatever" list.

The most drastic and usually the most effective remedy for fear is direct action. William Burnham

TOWARD THE OBSTACLES

I went whitewater rafting with my middle son Tyler when he lived in Montana. We wore our safety equipment and listened to the instructions of the guide as she told us what to do for particular circumstances.

One of the things she told us was, "When the raft goes up against an object, rock or tree, move quickly to that side." She said "to" that side, not away from it. We learned that if you move toward it, the water will come under the raft and roll it away from the obstruction. If you move away from the object, the raft lifts up on the object's side and can "dump truck" which means the raft tips up and "dumps" its contents, including you, into the water before flopping back down.

Hmmm, interesting. I think that same action applies to life as well. When you encounter an obstacle in your life maybe it's best to move "toward" it, acknowledge it and handle it. When you start "throwing your weight around" and attempt to move away from something that needs your attention, it may only serve to "up-set" everything or make things worse.

As much as I would have preferred to ignore my problems and hope they would go away, it didn't seem to happen. When I went toward my difficulties instead of running away from them, they weren't as powerful as I thought they were. I found out that standing up for myself and

21

handling what I would have preferred to ignore was strength building. And most of the time the work wasn't as difficult as I had imagined it would be. Okay, some of the time it was worse than I thought, but I am stronger for it.

Maybe there are other commonalities between whitewater rafting and life. There is the calm water and the standing waves. There sticking points and deep water, times you move slowly and times where it's swift. What if you accepted your quiet times *and* the more turbulent ones? What if you entered those rough waters with the same sense of exhilaration, of enjoying the ride that white water rafters do? How about deliberately concentrated on savoring the beauty surrounding you? What if you worked with others to carry the burdens or surrendered to the times when it was you who needed to be carried?

Here are some tips to ensure an enjoyable ride. Be safe, make suitable preparations, have the appropriate gear in good condition. You are the one who decides where you are going to put in and take out. Choose wisely good companions and a knowledgeable guide. Look around at the breathtakingly beautiful surroundings. Take photos and make memories to add to your *savorings* account to return to when you want.

Remember, life invites you to handle what's before you, your obstacles, sometimes by moving toward them, dealing with them straight on. Leaning into them may allow you to smoothly roll away.

When I think of water it reminds me of the childhood song *Row, Row, Row Your Boat.* There is deep wisdom in its pithy recommendations: *Row,* indicating there is work you need to do, so do it - paddle. It repeats this word a couple times - do the work, repeat, do the work. It is specific about whose boat - *Your* boat. Could that be as opposed to getting into someone else's business? Go *gently,* meaning the right strokes at the right time; sometimes on the right, sometimes on the left, sometimes not at all. *Down*-stream is suggested. Are you constantly going against the flow? If so, it might be time to rethink that. And three times the song exhorts *merrily*. Enter the joy that awaits you. Do you remember the final words: *life is but a dream*. When we're looking at our lives through spiritual eyes, there is so much more we can see beyond this material world. Also the song can be done in rounds. Take a part, add some harmonious companionship, and take turns.

The rafting company takes pictures at a particularly exciting spot on the river. The photos are great. There in the midst of the turbulent waves, most of us are smiling. Tyler, who had a shoulder injury not long before this trip, was not paddling. He's in the center of the raft with both hands to the sides of his face, mouth open, eyebrows raised pretending shock and fear. He was like that in all the pictures. Now, if it were *that* scary, he would at least be holding on *some* of the time. This points out even more choices. You can hold on, be afraid or you can let go and make funny faces.

What are the choices you make for your life? And most importantly, who it is you choose for a Guide?

 HERE'S ONE THOUGHT: I move toward my obstacles and handle them so they won't upset me.

Man need only divert his attention from searching for the solution to external questions and pose the one, true inner question of how he should lead his life, and all the external questions will be resolved in the best possible way. Leo Tolstoy

FOOTPRINTS IN THE SAND

Wintertime. Some people may think it's not the season to spend time at a New England beach. I beg to differ. You can take pleasure in the solitude of the beach. The crowds are gone and the beach is your own. When you're quiet, looking and listening, totally in the moment, you're open to new insights.

For over 25 years I lived in the New Hampshire seacoast area. Walking along "my" ocean beach one brightly sunny and bitterly cold winter day, the tide was out, and I noticed the ripples in the sand. Some were deep, some flat. The wind and water, the currents of life, can leave their mark. I could see it on the ocean sand and I could feel it in my heart. I had an awareness of the waves crashing into my heart, reaching into all the spaces and crannies and rearranging what was there. Like the rocks get moved on the beach, my heart was getting washed and renewed.

I saw footprints. Others had been here before me. There were deep footprints, widely spaced from people running, I presume. There were those that were less noticeable, closely spaced. I could imagine these belonging to someone treading lightly, going softly on the earth, maybe stepping slowly. There were large prints and smaller ones. I could even pick out certain individuals by the different patterns the tread marks of their soles left behind.

I saw more than people-prints. There were animal footprints too. Small ones scampering along beside a human print and larger ones with quick stops and starts, erratic, signs of playing. I imagined a small pup walking with its owner, or a large dog playing with a ball or a stick. I saw where birds had landed and run along the surf. I could tell the path the snails had traveled by the traces they left. Even things that don't move, the rocks and shells, left a hollowed out space around them where the water had moved the sand away. Everything appeared to make an impression.

It makes you wonder what marks you've left behind, and what those marks look like.

I looked back over my footsteps. Near me they were even and closely spaced. When I looked back over the entire beach, I noticed where I had jogged and twirled. I saw I had been meandering a little, walking toward a puddle, around a rock. Now looking back, I can remember the feelings of the slow time and the time of dance – the exhilaration of whirling with my arms in the air.

If you were to look back over the footprints of your past, what would you find? Think about it for a moment. Are there running steps? Softer footfalls? What other marks parallel or join yours? Are you stepping in another's tracks? Whose? What are you walking toward, away from or around? Is it how you wanted it to be? Can you imagine where someone might have carried you?

Winter. Sometimes it's the winter of my soul, a quiet time for greater insights, to look over where the currents of life, the marks of others and the steps I have chosen have

25

formed me. It's also a time to discern what my mission is, to uncover my deepest longings. A time to decide from the inner promptings: Who am I? Where do I go? Who do I travel with? What do I love? How do I walk on this earth? And what do I leave behind?

It came to me that the beach is new each day, a blank sheet, where the tide has washed it smooth *for-giving* me a new beginning. I have a fresh start daily to discover who I am, to make my marks and to leave the imprints of my choosing *...to dance with Life...to dance grace-fully.*

 HERE'S ONE THOUGHT: I have a fresh start each day, I begin again, anew.

*Hope is definitely not the same thing as optimism. It is
not the conviction that something will turn out well, but
the certainty that something makes sense, regardless of
how it turns out.* Vaclav Havel

SQUEEZING JOY OUT OF EVERY MOMENT

I had the pleasure of watching a private adoption of an infant baby for a friend who had always wanted to have a baby.

My friend excitedly showed me the ultrasound pictures and told me it was a girl. She hadn't shared the information about the adoption at her work or anywhere else in the community. She was worried something might happen, that it might not work out. I told her, "Go for it! Squeeze every drop of joy you can get out of it." I recommended that she tell everyone she knew, to enjoy the pleasure of each moment of thinking about it, and planning for it. Even if she were pregnant herself, something could happen to her baby. But right now all looked fine and she could choose to live in the present moment and embrace all the joy that can be found there.

What if later something did happen? If she told people about her joy now, they would find out about her loss too and be able to support her. Why is it that sometimes we choose to withhold comfort from ourselves? I know I have.

Fortunately, the adoption went through. She was at the hospital in the labor room to welcome her newborn daughter with dresses and other pink delights. Not everything goes as planned however (it was a boy) but HE has been a grand addition to that family.

I have found in my life that the most misery I've had has been self-inflicted. It comes from looking backward or forward, focused on what did happen to me that I didn't like, or what might happen to me that I didn't want. I was misusing my imagination for misery. When I had the grace to come back here and live in this moment, and then the next, everything was better.

Watch children. They live moment by moment. Sometimes we want them to behave differently, but maybe they're sharing their wisdom with us. It's a gift to be in the now. Actually, it's the only time we have – our present.

 HERE'S ONE THOUGHT: Let me squeeze all the joy I can out of *this* moment.

It turned out that this man worked for the Dalai Lama. And he said that they believe when a lot of things start going wrong all at once, it is to protect something big and lovely that is trying to get itself born – and that this something needs for you to be distracted so that it can be born as perfectly as possible. Anne Lamott

COW PLOP THEORY

One time, in response to a "How are you?" I answered, "I'm blossoming." Then the person wanted to know why I said that.

I didn't know. There was no particular reason except that I believe somehow it's happening all the time.

Anyway, they proceed to tell me about events in their life that they had judged as "bad" and it reminded me about the *Cow Plop Theory.*

The *Cow Plop Theory* is deep wisdom from my sister who has used it on me to pull me back in touch with reality. If you knew Irene you could hear her now: "Suppose you had a cow plop and you wished it were a birthday cake. It doesn't matter how long you wished it were a birthday cake, it's still a plop. You could put frosting on it. It's still a plop. You could put candles in it, light them and wish some more. It's still a plop. Maybe it's time to accept it and love it for what it "iz" – it's just fertilizer!"

Fertilizer? What if these "bad" circumstances are just the ones to help us grow?

I admit it. I don't really know how it's "supposed" to go. What I do know is that I've seen gifts come from circumstances that didn't look so pretty. And at times I don't remember this fact. What if this life is not about our financial, social or professional success? What if it's about soul growth? Then some of our most painful experiences have moved us furthest along our path.

Because I'm starting to trust in the all-rightness of life, I've resigned as general manager of the universe. Unfortunately, I've attempted to take up the job again on numerous occasions. I've had to quit multiple times now!

Back to the *Cow Plop Theory* and the birthday cake wish. Maybe the best thing is not for it to be cake. Maybe it's just what we need for growth in some area. When we see something coming at us that looks like manure, what if we called it fertilizer? Fertilizer for our soul. Then the "I'm blossoming" makes more sense.

Maybe that's where my initial comment that day came from – "I'm blossoming" – and so are you.

 HERE'S ONE THOUGHT: It's just *fertilizer*, watch me bloom and grow!

Death is not putting out the light. It is extinguishing the candle because the dawn has come. Unknown

MY DAD

They say people die as they live. Such was the case in my father's life and death. Both were gentle, peaceful, dignified and with grace. He had a rough last two years that included open heart surgery for bypass and valve replacement, a diagnosis of diabetes and then they found prostate cancer after it had already metastasized to his bones.

I remember when he had a section of his back removed and replaced with metal rods because the tumor was causing severe pain and would progress to paralysis and incontinence. Dad had valiantly attempted to regain all his pre-op activities. He was six-foot-four and around 220 pounds when he began his decline in the spring. He was walking with a walker, then used a game table chair with wheels to get around. Then he was in bed.

At first his strength would allow him to sit up on the side of the bed, and finally he couldn't even do that. He weighed less than 100 pounds while he was still able to stand and lost even more. It's painful to watch someone so well-loved prepare to leave you behind. I believe in miracles, so my energy was spent on prayers for a cure. Now I know there are other kinds of healing.

Dad was wise to the end, even when his physical strength was not sufficient for him to sit up in bed. I remember my niece was in high school at the time and she went to the funeral of a family member of one of her friends. Grandpa told her how proud he was of her, that it was important when someone is sorrowing to go to them and share in their sorrow. He also told her if she knew someone who was celebrating to go to them and share their joy. (What a better choice than envy.)

Even not eating and in constant pain, he was always "fantastic." I can still see his face light up when a couple came and shared the news that they were expecting a baby. Days before he died, he was genuinely so "glad to hear."

Shortly before Dad died, he said some words that we had to ask him to repeat; they were barely audible through lack of strength. I put my ear close to his lips and heard, "I am content." My cousin was there and explained that it is the title of a Lutheran hymn. Dad was Lutheran; I am Catholic. We later used that hymn at his funeral.

But as I have reconsidered those events, I don't believe Dad's comment on contentment was about that hymn at all. He had shared with us that the two most important things in life were one's faith and family. Dad was strong in his faith. He had told my mother she was a wonderful wife and they had wonderful children. He had told us that he loved us. I feel it was an attesting to the rightness of all, as Julian of Norwich said: *"All will be well, And all will be well, And all manner of things will be well."*

I believe in the quote at the top of the story and it gives me peace.

In your life, what thoughts do you hold onto? It's easy to have faith when everything seems right in your world. When crises or challenges come along, it is then more obviously the journey of your soul. That's the time to go deeper, praying for spiritual knowledge.

I, too, am content.

HERE'S ONE THOUGHT: I am content.

A man's concern, even his despair, over the worthwhileness of life is a spiritual distress but by no means a mental disease. It may well be that interpreting the first in terms of the latter motivates a doctor to bury his patient's existential despair under a heap of tranquilizing drugs. It is his task, rather, to pilot the patient through his existential crises of growth and development. Viktor Frankl

GROWING PAINS

Children are constantly growing. If there are children in your life whom you don't see on a regular basis, I'm sure you've noticed how "big" they've gotten since the last time you saw them. I remember a day when I noticed such a change in my youngest son. He looked taller than the last time I saw him. The unusual part about this was, that the last time I saw him was the night before when he went to bed. Now it was morning and he had literally "grown overnight."

In fact, at one time or another each of my children has cried or complained in the night of "growing pains." There wasn't much I could do. I used to rub their legs, but it didn't really seem to help. They were growing so much, they could feel it. And it hurt. Maybe the greatest help I could offer was just being awake with them, so they weren't alone with their pain.

Is it like that in your life? You may not be getting any taller but maybe you're still "growing" in some way, and sometimes it hurts. Is it because it's a time of rapid growth?

Would it easier to take it if you think your emotional or spiritual pain was due to rapid growth, an increase of your gifts?

"What gifts?"

"You've got to be kidding!"

"Where are they?"

"How could there possibly be gifts in *this* painful circumstance?"

Following a particular experience, ask yourself these questions: If I can find meaning in these troubles, would it help? Will my heart be more open to others? Is my compassion and understanding expanding? Will my ability to help others multiply? What if I am being prepared to do some great work? What if what I am going through will help equip me to perform some essential detail that will be important for the earth or just one other person? What if this experience qualifies me to know what to do for a loved one?

Would any of those answers make it any easier to take?

Just asking yourself those questions will start your mind on a search for the answers. And it usually finds something. Making meaning out of what's happening in your life, seeing the potential benefits, the gifts that might be hidden there, helps relieve some of your distress.

Meaning making is important.

And when you're in distress, it may help to find someone to sit with you.

 HERE'S ONE THOUGHT: I trust there's a gift in this experience somewhere. Where could it possibly be?

Lynn Durham

LISTENING

Most people don't know how to listen because the major part of their attention is taken up by thinking.
Eckhart Tolle

We have two ears and only one mouth. Could that be a reminder or recommendation to listen twice as much as we speak?

You have been given gifts to help guide your life: your mind, your body and your spirit. Like a compass they can help you stay on your path by giving warning signs to gently alert you when to make a course correction. It's your job to pay attention to these gifts. And when you give the gift of full attention to life, to others or yourself, it can be healing.

Would you start to pay attention if you knew it would help you feel better?

Just like your car has a warning light for low oil, we each have our own distress warning signs, symptoms or messengers that tell us we need a change. We're familiar with the physical signs: We've felt muscle tension and headache or other pains; we can feel our blood pressure or pulse rise or our breathing get rapid and shallow.

There are more than the physical signs. We might have a behavioral warning, like sleeping or eating too much or too little, or reaching for mood-altering substances. Our emotions could get volatile and cause relationship problems. We might even notice a sign of spiritual stress in apathy toward life or a cognitive warning when we feel it is difficult to think clearly. It's important to become aware of our own "usual" stress warning signs asking for our attention. Going back to the oil warning light - if it goes on there are several things we can do. We can ignore it, we can put electrical tape over the light so we don't see it, OR we can get oil.

This book is about thoughts. I invite you to listen carefully to your thinking. When you feel distressed, rewind the tape you've just heard and notice what you just said to yourself. Some of the worst terrorists in the world are between our ears. Have you noticed how mean you are to yourself at times? If someone heard you say those same words to another person, what would they think of you? Do you need some "mental" floss?

Becoming aware of what's happening is the first step. From there, we can decide where we want to go and then move in that direction. Maybe you want to challenge the thoughts that pop into your head. You may decide to be kinder and more gentle with your thoughts and words.

Did you know that your body is your friend? What is it trying to tell you? Is this body "messenger" the only way your soul can get your attention? As we increase our awareness, our body won't have to shout at us anymore.

You've heard of the "still, small voice." Sometimes life becomes so hectic that we don't take the time to be still and listen. If we would begin to stop and ask, "What is the best for all?" before charging ahead, I think we would find our lives and our world changing for the better. In each moment, a request for intuitive heart guidance can steer you in the right direction.

You already have the tools. Just sharpen them and practice the way you want to respond.

 HERE'S ONE THOUGHT: What's the best for everyone in this circumstance, and that includes me?

You give but little when you give of your possessions. It is when you give of yourself that you truly give. Kahlil Gibran

PRESENCE

It's no small thing to listen.

We are a people of marathons and movement. Being still is not one of our culture's fortes. We want our opinions heard and acknowledged.

We are fixers. It's difficult for me to listen without trying to fix or fade problems, when sometimes the greatest gift we can bring someone is our loving presence.

As a new graduate nurse, I worked at a VA hospital on a busy surgical unit. Some shifts it was difficult, if not impossible, to get everything done, never mind to have any spare moments. However, one day I managed to fit in a few minutes to sit with an older gentleman who had just had his second above-the-knee leg amputation.

He asked me why God didn't just let him die, and I sat down, rested my hand on his arm and listened. He recounted heartaches and named the physical challenges he and his family members faced. He railed against God as to why He would put so much disease and difficulty into one family. He felt he was no longer enough of a man to live with so much of his body missing.

I didn't know what to say. I cared. I wished there was something I could do to ease his pain. I wanted to fix it but I couldn't think of anything. What I did was to give him the gift of listening and being truly present with him.

One thing I do remember is asking him if he had children and grandchildren – an inspired thought, no doubt. I remember this because as he told me about them, his whole manner shifted and he beamed. It had seemed a remarkable change at the time.

I'm sure I would've had more recollection of those few minutes had I realized how important they were to this man at the time. And I probably wouldn't remember anything at all today if it were not for the fact that, weeks later, he walked over on two artificial legs from the rehabilitation unit with his wife to thank me. He thanked me, in his words, "for saving my life." He reminded me of the day I sat by his bed and listened. He told me that I had been instrumental in his desire to live.

What had I done? Nothing special. I merely sat with the man for a few minutes and listened. I wonder how many times I have missed an opportunity of allowing myself to be used to help someone heal their life. How little is asked of us at times.

Sometimes all it takes to make a difference are a few moments, a listening ear and an open heart.

 HERE'S ONE THOUGHT: Let me be here now, in this moment, a loving presence.

We can no longer stand at the end of something we visualize in detail and plan backwards from that future. Instead, we must stand at the beginning, clear in our intent, with a willingness to be involved in discovery.
Margaret Wheatley

DOING THE RESEARCH

Are you willing to experiment?
It could change your life.
All you have to do is: read and walk, sit and write, smile and help.

Block off twenty-four days and commit to change your life. Invest one hour a day. Break it down to suit your needs. Within one month, you will see a new world. And once discovered you'll never be the same again. What a difference those 24 hours will make!

Just as you need proper nutrition for your body to function well, you need proper nourishment for your mind to function well. Plan your mind food as you would your body food. Are you careful of what you feed your mind? If not, maybe it's time you begin.

Experiment in your life. Pick something, do it regularly and see what happens.

You can do affirmations. Affirmations are positive statements repeated with a feeling of desire. Use your mind power and the power of "feeling" to declare what you want to make "firm" in your life. If you want to use my "Prescription for Joy" bookmark, send me a self-addressed stamped envelope and I'll mail you one to use. (Find the address on my website www.LynnDurham.com).

Choose what you want to affirm and "take it" four times a day, like penicillin! You can use the 23rd Psalm or other sacred writing. Carry it with you, read it, say it out loud before each meal and before you go to bed. That won't take much time at all. You'll be planting these positive thoughts in your conscious and unconscious mind, and the repetition with feeling is like fertilizing and watering those seeds of change. Read an inspirational book at least ten minutes a day. You will be surprised at how effective this is.

Dr. Andrew Weil recommends fasting from news because of its negativity. Test it out, do the research and see what kind of effect that it has on you.

Walking, even if it's for ten minutes twice a day, will be beneficial. Can you park your car farther away in the store parking lot, walk to work or go out for a walk instead of taking a coffee break? When you go outside in nature, you have the benefit of the sunlight, and if you walk mindfully, paying attention to the sights and sounds around you, you can turn it into a walking meditation.

As you walk, release your negative thoughts and focus on the blessings of Mother Earth. Start, and you'll begin to notice small details you never saw before. When you concentrate and truly listen, you hear things that were there all along but had escaped your awareness. This shift of attention will change the experience of your walk.

Promise yourself you will sit for ten minutes twice a day. This is a time to just sit and listen. If ten minutes is too much, start with five.

Walk, read, be quiet. Commit to one small change. You don't have to believe me. Just investigate. See what happens when you make that change.

 HERE'S ONE THOUGHT: I am doing the research, experimenting in my life.

God has no hands or feet or voice except ours and through these he works. Teresa of Avila

THE STILL SMALL VOICE

I was at a conference and perched on my shoulder was a beautiful gold pin. At first glance it looked like an eagle, but it was a beautiful angel, wings outstretched, a unique design, unlike any I have ever seen before or since.

There's a little story about how it came to be there. My sister's friend Marcia was wearing it originally. My sister tells me she said, "That pin is great, where did you find it? I'd like to buy one for my sister, she loves angels." Marcia took it off and gave it to my sister to give to me. Wow! And I was blessed with this lovely gift.

At the break, a woman came up to me and said, "That pin is great, where did you find it? I'd like to buy one for my sister, she loves angels." And then...I heard a small voice say: *"Give her the pin."*

So naturally, I said to myself, "No, this was given to me" and I heard again, "Give her the pin." So of course, I told myself, "No, what would Marcia think if I just gave it away?" Once more I heard a little louder, "Give Her The Pin." And I thought, "It's a very unusual pin, how could I find another like it?" And then I heard a not so small voice yell, "GIVE HER THE PIN!" With a cringe I took it off and said out loud to the woman, "Here, give this to your sister."

She was surprised at first, asked me if I was serious [I don't think so] I said, "yes." When she said, "Are you sure?" I thought [this is my opportunity to get it back] and out of my mouth popped, "Yes." Then she said, "This is so wonderful, you don't know what this will mean to her, my sister loves angels, she has them all over her room, she's dying of cancer."

Hmmmmm.

Then I told her what I just told you, which made it even more meaningful to her and her sister and I released the pin with love.

By the way, I'm not just an easy mark to get my jewels, lots of people have complimented me on other pins and they didn't get them :-)

I believe things don't only come to us, but are supposed to pass through us to get to where they need to go. Maybe this includes more than things, maybe people come into our lives and go on, both blessing us and being blessed by our encounter, and are to be released in love.

Life is a circle. Things are not just going back and forth, but around and we play our part in moving things on in this dance of Life. Are you ready to let go with the flow? Are you listening to the small voice (or maybe not so small)? Do you say "NO!" or "YES!"?

 HERE'S ONE THOUGHT: I'm listening, what is it I'm to do?

The thing that is really hard, and really amazing, is giving up on being perfect and beginning the work of becoming yourself. Anna Quindlen

BEAUTIFUL IN OUR BROKENNESS

Shell. The definition is "the outer covering, hard case; or to remove from its shell or husk."

Carol Hamblett Adams, in her book *My Beautiful Broken Shell,* tells of walking along the beach one day during a particularly trying time in her life. She walks past a shell in search of the perfect one, then goes back, realizing "the shell is me with my broken heart, the shell is people who are hurting."

What if we are even more beautiful because of our brokenness? Maybe as the coverings break open or come off, they release our beauty that was encased in a hard shell. It's about becoming real, breaking out of our armor so the world can see we are beautiful. It's also about dropping off our judgments so we can see that the world is beautiful.

Jane Milotte makes shell jewelry. She takes the pieces and parts of shells that are sitting on the beach and assembles them into lovely pins. Broken shells that are mostly overlooked become charming ocean jewelry.

I have walked along the beach and helped add to her collection. I've noticed several things in this enterprise. First of all, I saw things I didn't noticed before when I briskly walked along the beach. The colors in the shells, once unseen, were amazing to me. Shells were blue, orange, bright purple,

47

rose, iridescent. They came in all shapes and sizes, and when I looked more carefully at them, I would see something like a hull or sail for a boat, a whale or fin, a butterfly or bird. I had never imagined the extent of discovery I would make about shell fragments.

More than the shells, I found that time changed for me. Busy with this venture, I walked farther, not noticing how the time flew by and the distance was easily traveled. I was surprised at how far I had come. I wonder, when we concentrate, does time literally expand?

When totally absorbed in this endeavor, there was no room for my whining or worries. Being mindful is good for my mental health and has physical health benefits that follow this good outlook.

Assembling of the pieces of broken shells into the finished pins took imagination, arrangement, gluing, backing and finishing to transform these overlooked chips of Neptune's bounty into beautiful creations. Broken parts of casing became attractive jewelry.

Maybe it's like that for us. We need to allow our shells to break open and embrace the pieces of our lives. We can transform through self-acceptance and welcome (gladly receive) these attractive gems.

When you realize your own beauty, you will also see beauty in others.

 HERE'S ONE THOUGHT: I am being shelled so my beauty can be released and I can see the splendor around me.

SERVING WITH LOVE

Everybody can be great, because everybody can serve.
You don't have to have a college degree to serve.
You don't have to make your subject and your verb
agree to serve. You don't have to know about Plato and
Aristotle to serve. You don't have to know Einstein's
theory of relativity to serve. You don't have to know the
second theory of thermodynamics in physics to serve.
You only need a heart full of grace, a soul generated by
love. And you can be that servant.
Martin Luther King, Jr.

Are you interested in having work you love? Do you wait for Friday, anxious to get out of a place where you spend many hours every week in misery? How can you change this? I have five suggestions: You can *locate, learn, buy, create,* and/or *love* your occupation.

Locate work you love; seek new employment, the "perfect" position, one that energizes you and gives you something to look forward to doing.

You also can *learn* a new profession, craft or trade. Educational opportunities and institutions abound. Even without leaving your home, you can take on-line or distance learning courses.

There is also the option of *buying* work you love. You could contact a business broker who can sell you an existing business. A man told me he enjoyed working long and hard and did it willingly when it was his own.

You can fashion work you love; *create* your own position. There are a vast array of careers and work opportunities from which to choose, and there is also the potential to envision a new one.

Or...you can make your work *love* – right here, right now. When you change your mind set to "How can I serve?" there are all sorts of benefits. Check out the Institute for Research on Unlimited Love.

 HERE'S ONE THOUGHT: I think I'll be of service - it's just a selfish thing to do.

The most important thing in life is to learn how to give out love, and to let love come in. We think we don't deserve love, we think if we let it in we'll become too soft... Love is the only rational act. Mitch Albom

WE ARE GIFTS TO EACH OTHER

I remember a patient I cared for many years ago when I was a student nurse on Pediatrics. He was a young boy who had valiantly fought leukemia for many years. He had been in and out of the hospital on many occasions, and the staff knew him and his parents well.

This young boy was receiving treatment in the hopes of another remission, but it didn't seem to be working this time and he had gone into a coma. Each day, his mother would come, and after he was washed and changed, he would be carefully moved into his mother's waiting arms in a rocking chair next to the bed, IV running.

It had been over a week since he had last responded when he surprised his mother by regaining consciousness while in her arms. He looked up at her and said, "I love you, Mommy." Then he closed his eyes and left this world.

I remember thinking that the staff's role "should" be to console the grieving family. Yet, in this case it seemed to be the other way around. The mother and father had come to terms with the fact that this time there might not be another remission; the staff had not. After all, it's their job to find the cure and defend against death, isn't it? I'm glad everyone doesn't look at it that way anymore.

What I saw was the family consoling the staff. The parents shared how they couldn't have asked for a more beautiful way for their angel to leave them. They shared their deep faith and their love with those nurses they had come to know and appreciate.

Maybe things don't only move in one direction. Sometimes we are the giver, the server, the nurturer, and sometimes the receiver, the served and the nurtured. No matter our role, in order to be whole, it's important to be open to both giving and receiving.

Truly, we are gifts to one another.

 HERE'S ONE THOUGHT: I am open to giving AND to receiving.

I can only love one person at a time. I can only feed one person at a time. Just one, one, one... So you begin...I begin. I picked up one person – Maybe if I didn't pick up that one person, I wouldn't have picked up 42,000... Same thing for you, Same thing in your family, Same thing in your business. Wherever you go just begin...one, one, one. Mother Teresa of Calcutta

UNDERWHELMED WITH OVERWHELMED

Are you overwhelmed with things to do?

Consider a highway construction project. Does the road crew ever get overwhelmed when they're building a new road? Do they whine and complain, "Oh, I have so much to do"? For certainly there is a lot for them to do to complete such a task.

I doubt the workers on road projects whine about the size of the job before them. They just do it – one shovel at a time, by hand or by vehicle, one and one and one. In fact, I've heard they're actually glad there's a lot to do. They look at it differently. After all, it will keep them employed for a long time. What if we looked at everything we have to do that way? "I'll be needed here because there's a lot for me yet to do."

Whenever I've had the grace to shift from all I have to do and look at the next small task at hand, I relax in mind and body. I accomplish more in that state. It feels better and is better for me. When my vision gets diffused on too many things, I don't get much of anything done. When I have a lot to do and start to terrorize myself with my thoughts, I think

53

about the highway workers and how they don't seem to be overwhelmed. I bring my scattered thoughts in and focus only on the next thing to do, and then the next, and the next, and more seems to get accomplished.

There's something else I've noticed about road projects. Once when I was driving my son to school, crews were working on the turnpike. I could see that someday I would drive through on the new road and not have to stop at the traffic light. For months we watched the workers busy with the construction progress. Then one day, I noticed I hadn't gone through the light. I had traveled the new road for the first time, but I didn't observe the change until later. I had driven where it seemed natural to go.

Maybe that's what it's like when we are making a change for ourselves. We need to practice and work one shovelful at a time and then another. We make plans, keep building and working at it, maybe poorly at first, until one day we find it just happens naturally. We had intended the change, but then we didn't even notice when it occurred.

I believe in miracles that happen in a moment, and I know that some miracles take time. With focus, we can move closer to our goal one thought and one action at a time. We can create new pathways for ourselves and complete tasks that seemed so daunting to us at first.

Be at peace, all is well, just keep doing.

 HERE'S ONE THOUGHT: I am focused on doing my next task, on completing my next small step.

Our business in life is not to succeed, but to continue to fail in good spirits. Robert Louis Stevenson

POORLY AT FIRST

The first time I heard, "If something is worth doing, it's worth doing poorly at first," I was surprised. I thought about it for a while and now I see the truth of it. If something is important enough, it's important to get it started, such as it is.

In fact, perfectionism can be used as an excuse to procrastinate. My friend Dr. Patt Schwab, a humorist from Seattle, says, "Procrastination is a form of perfectionism." She's also of the opinion, "as long as you're going to "crastinate," you might as well be a pro!"

Whenever you are learning a skill, whether it's tying your shoes or playing the piano, your first attempts are not that great. You try it anyway, and you keep practicing. And it gets better. How good can you be at anything the first time you do it? If you have a more relaxed view of life, the task will get done and be brought to the light of day, even if it isn't "perfect."

If you are painting the house or painting a picture, it's one brush stroke and then another and another until you're done. What if you could enjoy the pleasure of the moment? I have seen people unwilling to attempt something because they didn't think they would do it well. Why do we think we can do something well the first time? But what if your priority were joy and not perfection?

There is a blessing that says, "May you be blessed with the gift of *enough.*" Enough can take many forms. It could be that you feel there is enough time, that something is good enough, that you have enough, or that you are enough. It's the gift of contentment. It's fine to have dreams and to work for more AND also to know that it's all right now.

Contentment isn't about settling; it's about honoring the process. It doesn't eliminate possibilities for moving toward perfection in the future. Contentment is gratitude for what you've been given now, even knowing there is still possibility for growth and change.

In doing this book, I'm going to have to stop editing and get it to a printer. Out it will come, such as it is. If you are reading this in book form, I did it. You might think, "She should have worked on it some more." There are always new editions, but right now, this is good enough.

 HERE'S ONE THOUGHT: I am blessed with enough. My priority is not perfection; it's joy!

We should not think that holiness is based on what we do but rather on what we are, for it is not our works which sanctify us but we who sanctify our works.
Meister Eckhart

ALL JOBS ARE IMPORTANT

Sometimes we wonder what our mission in life is. We go on, day after day, doing routine things and think that what we do is not important. But as we go about our business, we are touching others and may never know what kind of effect we are having.

That's how it was with a friend of mine, Nan. She was working in a credit union where she ran the checking department. Nan worked in a separate glassed-in office space when she was interrupted by a large, muscular young man. Lenny had stomped through the department, thrown open the door, stood glaring at her for a moment in the doorway, and then entered, slamming the door behind him so all the glass partitions shook. Nan could see the concerned faces of the tellers wondering if they should call for help.

With her eyes she told the others "no" and turned to look at Lenny. His neck veins were distended. He demanded to know why they were bouncing his checks. She was surprised that she didn't feel afraid. She offered him a seat and asked if she could see his checkbook register. She told him she would pull up his account on the computer to see if they could find the problem. He told her he didn't have one and pointed to his head, saying, "I keep it all up here."

She didn't laugh. She told me she doesn't know where it came from but she said, "I bet you work shift work, days, nights, swing." He said, "Yes." Then she asked, "Do you work overtime?" Another yes. "You're tired, aren't you?" He nodded. Nan said, "I don't know how you could remember every check you wrote. I couldn't. Maybe that's the problem."

So sitting together, she took out a blank checkbook register, printed his statement and taught Lenny how to balance a checkbook. They were together about two hours. His name never came across her desk for overdrafts again.

Many of us wonder what good we are doing in the world, repeating many of the same tasks daily. Knowing Nan, I'm sure she has lifted more people than she knows. She could have laughed that anyone would attempt to remember all the checks they wrote. She treated Lenny only with kindness, compassion and respect.

She wouldn't have known what a difference she made except for a letter she received one day, months later, from Lenny's mother. She was writing to thank Nan for all the help she had given her son that day. Nan said, "Lenny had told his mother all about me, what I had done that day and how nice I had been. She told me how proud he was that he never bounced another check. And then she told me that Lenny had been killed in a car accident, and she wanted to thank the people who had been kind to him."

Nan continued, "In those days, I wasn't thinking, 'What is my purpose?' but I found a part of that answer anyway. I could be of service to people beyond pushing paper." What strikes me is that Nan would never have known what impact she'd had on that young man's life if it weren't for the letter she received from his mom. Whether we are aware of it or not, we may deeply affect those with whom we come in contact in so many ways.

What kinds of interactions do you have with others? What would they say about you? Another question I have is: Is there anyone you could tell about the impact they've had on your life? It might be important to them. Being kind and acknowledging others for their kindnesses, that sounds like a good way to live to me. And it spreads. You are contagious. Peace begets peace, love more love and joy spreads joy. What is it that others catch from you?

 HERE'S ONE THOUGHT: How can I best make this interaction more positive?

59

Do not allow yourselves to be disheartened by any failure as long as you have done your best. If you are discouraged, it is a sign of pride because it shows you trust in your own powers. Never bother about people's opinions. Be humble and you will never be disturbed.
Mother Teresa of Calcutta

MASHED POTATOES

When I was teaching a course on the *Psychology of Success*, the book had many personal exercises to complete. I gave the assignments and told the students to write exactly what they felt, and that I wouldn't read what they wrote. I would only check that the pages were filled with writing. One of my students said her son had asked her, "You mean if you wrote "mashed potatoes" the teacher would think you did the work?"

Yes, they could have written "mashed potatoes" or whatever they wished. I would have seen the writing and checked off that they had completed the work. But who loses? Certainly not I.

Now I would love for all my students to get As. I have been thanked by students when they received an A. But I don't deserve thanks for that any more than blame if someone gets an F. By claiming responsibility for their actions, or non-actions, that created those grades in their courses, students empower themselves to know they can make the necessary adjustments that will alter the grading results.

How much is it like that for the rest of life? We can slide by. Or we can do the work. When we do less than is required, we diminish ourselves energetically and in our self-esteem. Sometimes the work is hard. Self-examination is not always easy. Yet, when we are willing to put forth the effort, we learn, we grow and we feel the satisfaction of a job well done. When something doesn't happen as you wished, yet you know that you did the best you could, you have no regrets for your actions and can feel more at peace. What do you want for yourself?

As I was reading the final exam, I noticed that the student mentioned above started one of her essay question answers with the words "mashed potatoes." It made me laugh, as I'm sure she smiled inside as she wrote it. Then she went on to answer fully the challenge set before her.

I have often reminded my students that they aren't in school for a letter grade, that the alphabet does not name their worth. They have been called to study in order to learn. "Learner" is their vocation at this point and I encourage them to be the best in their chosen career.

Are you willing to do the work? Or is it "mashed potatoes" for you?

 HERES ONE THOUGHT: I am doing my best, even if no one else knows, because I do, and it's important to me.

No habit is so important to acquire as the ability to delight in fine characters and noble actions. Aristotle

GETTING THE GOODS ON THEM

Have you ever considered sharing messages of love, even at work? Working with a company to shift some of the negativity, I assigned an exercise to a team. They were given these instructions to help build morale and cohesiveness:

List your coworkers and then consider each one carefully. Look deeply. Uncover their strengths, gifts and what they add to the workplace and to your life. Shift from any judgment you might hold, turn from their challenges and focus on what you appreciate about them. I challenge you to find as many things to affirm about your least favorite person as you do your most favorite. Take some time and consideration. Keep this mission at the top of your mind as you go about your work, focusing on their best selves. Then you decide what to put down on paper for them. I will take your words of kindness and support and compile them for each person. Thank you. You're a great group and I hope you can see all the beauty.

There were eleven in the group. They were looking at and considering all the same people. There was one person who had difficulty finding good things to write about almost everyone. "Comes to work on time" was the best they could do for one person. And for another it was, "acts childish." Yet, someone else in the group could make a long list of good things for everyone. He didn't have enough room on the paper to list all the good he saw in each co-worker. Where are those attributes, in the person or the observer? Interestingly, everyone else had good things to say about him too.

Eventually, over the course of the program, there was a change in perception. The group that entered the multi-week wellness process did not emerge the same. As people began to consciously look for the good, they began to find it. A strong feeling of kindness and cohesiveness developed within that group.

When you were in school you probably looked into a microscope. When I first did I saw a white circle. That's all I could see until I turned the knob and changed the focus. And then a whole world of squiggling things was revealed. They were always there, just out of focus.

So I invite you to set your intention to find the beauty in others and in yourself. What if you shifted your focus and celebrated the loveliness you found and then told the others about what you discovered?

We even have the month of February designated to remind us of hearts and love. Will you open your heart, and just like breathing, let the love flow – in and out – to all those in your life?

 HERE'S ONE THOUGHT: I am focusing on the good in others...and myself.

Lynn Durham

BLESSINGS OF CHILDREN

The teacher, who is indeed wise does not bid you to enter the house of his wisdom but rather leads you to the threshold of your mind.
Kahlil Gibran

Adults think we need to be the teachers for our children. I would say that many times the children are great teachers for us.

I was "reading" a Richard Scarry book with my son Brett when he was a toddler. I would point to one of the wonderful pictures and tell him what it was or ask him to tell me. He had a limited vocabulary and it was expanding.

One day he seemed to be stuck on the word "dog." I'd point to an airplane and he'd say dog. I'd say "airplane." Then on to a dump truck; he called it a dog, I would correct him. My finger landed on a boat; again he said dog, and I started to say boat when I looked more carefully. The driver of the boat was a dog. I looked back and in the tiny windows of the truck and plane, there sat ... a dog! Brett was looking more closely than I was. He was right!

When we choose to look from the angle of a child, we just may see something else. Maybe they're seeing something we're missing. Maybe God has something He wants us to see and will use our children to lead us. If we can suspend our view for a moment and attempt to look at what they're seeing, we may find something new. Something that was always there but we had missed it.

 HERE'S ONE THOUGHT: How does this look from their angle?

Sometimes I go about pitying myself, and all the time I am being carried on great winds across the sky.
Ojibway Dream Song

OUT OF THE MOUTHS OF BABES

One day following my separation I was afraid and sad. My youngest son noticed and asked me what was wrong. I sighed and told him, "Josh, I don't know where we're going to live."

He jumped up on my lap, put his little arm around my neck and said, "But, Mom, they have places for homeless people, don't they?"

His optimistic hopefulness washed over me and made me smile.

It put things in perspective for me. No, I wouldn't need a homeless shelter. I had friends and family who would take me in before I needed to go there. And on the other hand, that there were such places is a great blessing as well, filled with kind and loving people there to help.

I heard Carolyn Myss describe how her family would take a "misfortune," and go around the table, taking turns making it worse each time. Her example was a relationship "at least you didn't...or he didn't...(fill in the blank), until by the time the tale made it's way back to her she was relieved that it occurred just the way it did and grateful that was all that had happened.

Sometimes the thoughts of how things could be worse help us to accept what is. Sometimes this exercise shows us we have blown things out of proportion. I know that when I've shifted my focus back to the blessings, things didn't seem so bad and I felt much better.

 HERE'S ONE THOUGHT: This could be worse.

During [these] periods of relaxation after concentrated intellectual activity, the intuitive mind seems to take over and can produce the sudden clarifying insights which give so much joy and delight. Fritjof Capra

THE 3 R'S OF RESILIENCE

We want the best for our children. What can we give them as tools for life? How about teaching the 3 R's of resilience: relax, reflect, and respond. When the stress response is elicited, I've mentioned a number of negative things that happen physically in the body. We can change what happens in our body by changing our thoughts, words and actions in the moment.

We have a choice. We get to determine the thoughts we'll hold, when we'll speak, what we'll say, in short, how we'll respond – our respondability. Responsibility - choosing our response to any situation.

The Education Initiative from the Harvard Deaconess Mind Body Medical Institute, now known as the Benson Henry Institute of Mind Body Medicine at Massachusetts General Hospital, has done research on the relaxation response and academic achievement. They used the four measures of grade point average, work habits, cooperation and attendance. They found that students taking their relaxation based program had improvement in academic performance, work habits, memory, self-esteem and a decreased perception of stress.

I've had my children listen to relaxation tapes and experience how it feels as they consciously let go and calm down. I've led guided visualizations for students in schools. Children enjoy using their imaginations. Learning to take slow, deep breaths is an important technique for being more peaceful.

Children can choose AND they watch and learn from you. Do you *Relax* into the moment with a deep breath? Do you *Reflect* on what is most kind and respectful? Do you choose to *Respond* (take response-ability for your thoughts, words and actions as opposed to blaming others) or are you a reactor on automatic (with a mushroom cloud?) pretending that others are the cause of how you live your life?

I remember my middle son saying a bad word in junior high. When I told him it was not acceptable he explained it wasn't his fault. Why? Because he heard that word all the time, in school, on the bus, etc. I told him I was going to let him in on a powerful secret. It would be a life altering awareness. I told him he was the only one who moved his tongue that formed the words that came out of his mouth. Everyone is blaming everyone else for their own words and actions. When we realize who is responsible, that we have a choice in each moment, the ability to respond, it gives each individual back their power.

To really teach it to the children, we have to do it ourselves. Resources are abundant. You can get a coach, take a workshop, buy a CD and practice new skills. It's important for your health – physical, mental, emotional and spiritual. Practice the 3 R's of resilience - relax, reflect and respond. It's a gift for yourself, for your children and for all those you touch.

Remember ...the children are watching you.

 HERE'S ONE THOUGHT: Am I using the 3 R's – relax, reflect, respond?

I cannot but have reverence for all that is called life. I cannot avoid compassion for everything that is called life. That is the beginning and foundation of morality.
Albert Schweitzer

THE WAY OUT AND THE WAY IN

I was walking by a weeping willow tree one day and stopped to look at the leaves. I didn't remember touching a weeping willow since I was a child. We used to have one in our yard in Lordship, Connecticut. And hanging on, in clumps and piles, were Japanese Beetles. I remember the beetles well. I wasn't afraid to touch them. In fact, I used to "train" them to walk along popsicle sticks. (Where else were they going to walk when on a stick?)

I did not, however, like them in my hair, which was long and curly, well, "frizzy" might be a better description. Getting them in the girls' hair was the boys' favorite pastime. And with my thick locks, it was not always easy to get those beetles out. Funny how one thought will trigger another memory.

Stopping to touch the weeping willow leaves reminded me of my childhood days spent being in the moment and connecting with nature in the long joyful days of summer. Children are natural experts at that.

I have a challenge for you, for those who walk and/or exercise outside and for those who would be willing to walk this week. Take your walk, stroll, jog as you normally would,

71

to the point where you turn back. Then as you return, I want you to do it mindfully. If you're with someone, explain what you're doing. You can invite them to participate.

To walk back mindfully, stop talking, turn off your radio and come to awareness of your senses, all of them. Turn up and tune in to your hearing, feeling, smelling, and seeing. Notice the sounds that were below the level of your awareness the first time you passed by. Stop and smell a planting or flower; touch one and feel the temperature and texture; notice the veins in the leaves, the insects on the ground; feel the sun or wind on your face. Feel the gratitude for the wonders of nature and the miracles of your body. Perceive everything.

When you get back home, compare the way out and the way in. "Way in" is a good term. It's the way in to another world. I would be interested to hear from anyone about their experiences. Write to me at the snail mail or email address on my website www.lynndurham.com

I know I experienced this exercise. I was in Boston and did not notice the birds when I walked out. Even the traffic sounds were not so noticeable on the way out as they were on the way in. I also noticed the plantings and earthy smells mingled with the traffic odors. The warmth of the sun and the feel of the wind on my face were also lost to me until I turned up my awareness. And in doing so I could feel myself relax.

Sometimes in our daily life, we get so involved and rushed. We want to hurry our children along too. But they are natural explorers, distracted by what we judge as "unimportant" things like bugs and leaves and sticks that could float as pretend boats. We may think they're "trying" to make us late. I have a couple of recommendations. One is to leave earlier so you have more time to wander. The other is to think positive thoughts about your children. Love them for being your teachers, for being experts in looking at life.

Acknowledge what they see and share their experience. Tell them that next time you'll leave extra early because you want to see what they have to show you.

Then do it.

 HERE'S ONE THOUGHT: I cherish this child; s/he is just reminding me to live more mindfully.

We all live in suspense, from day to day, from hour to hour; in other words, we are the hero of our own story.
Mary McCarthy

BONE MARROW BIOPSY

When my middle child, Tyler, was a toddler, he was often sick. I think his spleen was slightly displaced. Doctors had noticed an irregularity when he was born. But because he was a blond-haired, blue-eyed boy, with an enlarged spleen, frequent sicknesses, unusual blood picture and a bruise on his belly, his pediatrician called me one night with the information that she felt it important to have a bone marrow biopsy. She didn't say it was leukemia, but if it might be, there was more success if it were treated early.

What kind of things go through a mother's mind when she hears such a possibility? I didn't feel that it was true, but that a doctor wanted to check it out was very scary. Fortunately, the appointment was the following morning and I didn't have a lot time to stress. I don't always take my own advice but in fleeting moments of clarity when I've been wise enough to do what I say – I've found it to work! I'm practicing too.

We went to the special clinic at the Massachusetts General Hospital in Boston. As I sat in the waiting room with many other parents and children, I wondered about their children. My oldest son, Brett, was busy asking what the marks were on the face of a young child. The parents patiently explained it was so the technicians would know where to focus the radiation. One toddler had an IV in his arm. He was playing happily until they called his name, then he immediately began screaming. As I heard the calls for radiation and chemotherapy, saw the marks and tubing, and talked to the parents, I found out that we were the only family that was not yet diagnosed. People had traveled from great distances to have their children treated at this center.

Another mother surprised me with the comment, "Oh, that was the worst part, the waiting and wondering." I was reminded of the quote from the English novelist Anna Sewell, "I am never afraid of what I know." And a friend's comment, "I can handle anything, Lord, just give me the strength." That mother shared she could handle what she needed to do; she just needed to know what she was dealing with.

I was thinking, "I would rather be wondering than knowing what she knew about her child." They ran the test on Tyler right away. There was only a short wait and we got the results. He checked out OK. He didn't have cancer. An ear infection was the culprit for the increase in white cell count and I didn't realize they thought the monkey bite his brother had given him on the belly was spontaneous bruising. We didn't need to join that group of parents and children, and I was so grateful.

This incident brought things into perspective for me. I became more thankful about a lot of things. Our old car was just fine even if it had trouble starting sometimes. I thought that our small home was larger than many of the world's people could even imagine. We had food, our health and our family.

Why did it take such a scare to bring me back into the place of gratitude? Why do I wander so quickly into focusing on what I lack? How about you? What thoughts do you need to have to keep you living in appreciation? Whatever they are for you, find them and use them regularly to keep you in the state of gratefulness.

Even as I write this, I see how I had been looking in the wrong direction. I am now opening my heart to the blessings in my life and turning away from the negativity. All I have to do is ... reread my writings, listen to my tapes and follow my instructions!

You decide what is right for you and what is right for this moment.

 HERE'S ONE THOUGHT: What thought can I hold that will bring me to peace about my current situation, in this moment?

Each day of our lives we make deposits in the memory banks of our children. Charles Swindoll

CLOTHES FOR PAJAMAS

Is Love the touchstone of your life? Is it the primary goal for your relationships? I remember one day having a disagreement with my youngest son. He was a little guy, and he was so slow in getting ready and out the door in the mornings. I didn't want to be late for work. Has this ever happened in your life?

My preferred way of being in this world is to go kindly, gently and joyfully, living in love. Contrary to this intention, I started to yell at him about getting ready faster. Then I remembered my heart's desire and stopped. Maybe my conscious "choice of being" awakened me to the fact that I was not in alignment with my goal. I asked myself, "What is it I most want him to know?" My answer: that he is loved. More specifically: that I love him. It was a moment of grace.

Then I asked myself: "Does this help me toward that goal?"

"Definitely not!"

In circumstances such as these, what if we take up the mirror and ask: "How can *I* make this better?" We are all extremely creative, and as we use our creativity we get more so. What if we look at our particular situation from every angle? What are all the things influencing this? What are all the possible solutions?

77

One solution immediately came to mind. If my little guy needs more time to get ready, then we'll have to get up earlier. Noticing that changing out of his pajamas and into his clothes was a hassle, another idea was to get him more ready for school at night. He liked wearing sweat suits to school. So, at night after his bath, instead of PJ's, he put on a clean shirt and clean sweat pants that he could wear to day care.

I must admit I felt a little guilty at the time, like I was being a "bad mother." The question, "What will other people say?" ran through my mind. But when we were up a few minutes earlier, we had snuggle time and I could read to him. So, that's what we did. I found that awakening slowly and having fun together before he got up, started the day on a better note. I know I felt better about our mornings.

When the story was finished and I said we had to get up and ready, it was okay with him, and dressing was expedited because he was mostly dressed. Now it was easy for him and easy for me to get downstairs for a pleasant breakfast together.

I have no doubt that this slight change in our routine influenced the rest of our day as well. In later years, he got himself up and dressed, and was not late for most of the rest of his school days.

I think we need to hold onto that touchstone of love. I recommend we live more aware and wake up to what's going on in that moment. If we are willing to be creative and to initiate change if necessary, our lives will go more smoothly. What's your intention of how to live your life? How does that intention influence your behavior in your moments? When you hold up your actions to the touchstone of love, how do they measure up?

HERE'S ONE THOUGHT: Is this action in alignment with my hope for our life together and what I most want them to know?

Not everything that can be counted counts, and not everything that counts is counted. Albert Einstein

ANN'S BABY

I have a friend, Ann, who had always longed to have a baby. She and her husband, Ray were blessed to have two school-aged children come into their lives and hearts. They loved the boys as their own. Still they continued to seek adoption of an infant but hadn't been successful. They never gave up hope and, for twelve years, prayed daily for their infant.

Sarah, an early high-school student, was unmarried, pregnant and afraid. Her parents both worked and didn't have a lot of money. Their health policy at that time only covered spousal maternity costs.

Through an intermediary, Ann and Ray asked if Sarah would be open to giving her baby to a good home - theirs. Sarah and her parents said they would consider it but first they wanted to meet the couple. Prior to the meeting, Ann and Ray made a photo album of their entire extended family. They showed Grandpa's farm and the other family homes where the baby would visit. Ann's now teenage sons each wrote a letter saying how thrilled they would be to welcome a new sibling into their lives.

I wonder what went through that young girl's mind as she made her choice. Why did Sarah not come to the most frequently chosen option of abortion? What did it take to consider carrying that pregnancy to term, delivering a beautiful newborn and then letting her child go? It must leave a tear in any mother's heart to think of this.

Maybe Sarah thought of what she had to offer this child at her young age and compared it to the loving family that could welcome her child. Whatever process she went through, it was a hard decision and a loving choice. Sarah said yes. She decided to have "Ann's baby."

I say it that way because Sarah began to think and talk of the child in such terms. It must be far easier to give up your child to a somewhat known environment. The young mom appeared to have started the emotional detachment process well before it happened physically. Sarah took comfort in knowing where her baby would go; some of what her baby would be doing, and who her baby would be with.

As Sarah and her child's future parents visited and got to know each other, a bond was formed. Ann and Ray picked out names for a boy and a girl and shared them with the teens family. Ann supported Sarah during her pregnancy and offered to be with her in labor and delivery. When the time came to deliver, Ann and Ray drove the distance to be there. Ray got to pace in the father's waiting room with the other expectant dads while Ann assisted in the labor room.

At one point, the baby's heart stopped beating. They had to perform an emergency caesarian section. Sarah was distraught at the thought of Ann losing her baby. Ann and Ray were extremely upset, not only about the possibility of losing their baby, but also about the well-being of this courageous young woman – a child who could have been one of their own, a teenager they had come to love.

Sarah's mom went with her for the surgery. Ann and Ray waited right outside the delivery room door and heard their baby's first cry. Several minutes later, Sarah's mother came out with the doctor and said to him, "Doctor, I'd like you to meet Joshua's mother and father." And with that, both Ann and Ray broke into tears of joy.

Baby and "mothers" were fine. A mom, a dad, two brothers and baby were together because a mother's heart was so full it only wished for the well-being of her child.

Maybe it isn't a tear in the heart at all. Maybe it's just an opening where more love can flow through ... onto everyone there, onto everyone who knows this story and onto everyone Joshua touches.

 HERE'S ONE THOUGHT: What is the most loving thing I can do for all involved?

Always be faithful in little things, for in them our strength lies. To God nothing is little. He can not make anything small; they are infinite... Do not pursue spectacular deeds... What matters is the gift of your self, the degree of love that you put into each one of your actions. Mother Teresa of Calcutta

LUNCH BOX LOVE NOTES

Everyone has lots of stories to tell, and I love to hear people tell them. The truth in the fabric of the tales goes more directly into our texture than any lists or rules ever could. Our stories have wisdom woven through their words and we don't even have to be aware of the wisdom for it to affect us.

At one recent program I was presenting, a single mom came up to me and shared a tradition she started when her daughter entered school. It can be difficult for little ones to remember where they're to go after school when their schedule changes. To help her daughter remember Joyce wrote a note to Julie every day and put it in her lunchbox. It was a love note and a reminder of what was happening that day. It could say, "Come home directly on the bus. I love you" or "You are wonderful! I'll pick you up after soccer." Other notes may have been, "I'm proud of what you are doing in school," or there might be a drawing of flowers with the note, "I'm sending you a bouquet of Love" or "You looked very nice when you went to school this morning."

I think it's a great idea. How nurturing for our children to get those special words and what a relief for them to know what they need to do that day.

But that wasn't the reason Joyce was telling me. She was remembering a day when she was sick. Julie was in sixth grade at the time, and she told her mother to stay in bed, that she would fix her own lunch that day, which she did. What amazed Joyce was that included in the lunch bag was a note, "I love me. Go home on the bus."

Joyce mentioned it because she wished she could have written such a note when she was twelve years old. I love to tell this story because I think it's a great tradition, and it appears to be working to help Julie, a special needs child, feel secure by knowing what to do.

It may be easy to get involved in the big, expensive things we do for our kids and neglect the small things that may count the most. What are some of the little things you will do to help your children know they are loved?

 HERE'S ONE THOUGHT: What can I do to let my child better know that I love them?

CHERISHING EACH OTHER

*One looks back with appreciation to the brilliant
teachers, but with gratitude to those who touched our
human feelings. The curriculum is so much necessary
new material, but warmth is the vital element for the
growing plant and for the soul of the child.*
Carl Jung

In *The Heart's Code*, Dr. Paul Pearsall talks about the study of "energy cardiology" which draws upon physics and cardiology and modern systems theory. Since ECGs (electrocardiograms) and MCGs (magnetocardiograms) are measured outside the body, this means it travels from the heart to the skin. And then what? He says, "Simple physics tells us that energy and information leave the body and go out into space." In his book he suggests that the heart thinks, feels and cells remember. He cites numerous examples of heart transplant patients "knowing" things about their donors and that there is a powerful non-local energy that is connecting everything and everyone. He calls it "L energy." This can give us a different view of health and healing, a way of looking at well-being that includes spiritual balance. This research can be the answer to those who ask, "What's Love got to do with it?"

Dr. Pearsall also suggests "that the heart is the conductor that keeps all the cells playing the same score." Music is not just something you hear, it may become the vibrational medicine of the future. Don Campbell, author of *The Mozart Effect*, talks about particular sounds, tones and rhythms, strengthening the mind, unlocking creative energies and even healing the body. Heal means to cure or make sound again, as sound is synonymous for health and wholeness. You don't even have to hear to listen to music. Beethoven was only one of history's great musicians who had been deaf. Somehow, he perceived the "rhythmic codes and patterns through the vibrations he felt in other parts of his body."

Evidence continues to mount proving the importance of "loving" on the quality of our life and health. The Institute of HeartMath, Boulder Creek, California, has shown the close relationship between our mental and emotional attitudes and the heart's electrical system. HRV (Heart Rate Variablity) Patterns that are random and jerky are typical of someone feeling frustrated or distressed. The good news is people can neutralize and shift this pattern into a more ordered and harmonious pattern by recalling sincere feelings of love, care, or appreciation. Negative emotions are draining. When you notice frustration, they recommend "Freeze-Frame" where you take a time out, feel with the heart, remembering a positive feeling and ask what a more efficient response would be. Your heart knows. They have the documentation to prove that re-experiencing the positive feeling of Love is biologically beneficial and can help you in the moment.

Dr. Dean Ornish, author of *Reversing Heart Disease*, has also written *Love and Survival: The Scientific Basis for the Healing Power of Intimacy*. In it he details study after study that show how important supportive connections are in wellness and longevity. He originally thought it was the exercise programs and dietary changes that were so effective. And while taking care of your physical needs for rest, exercise, nutrition, and healthy choices are important, he also knows the significance of the love given and received unconditionally in the support groups. So many times, we are looking for love, but love is all around us. If we love ourselves and others we feel it first as it flows through us. One of the ways to get out of a depression is to look for someone else to help. In serving we benefit, in giving we receive.

Spirit is the cutting edge in all areas of life. Some people need to have "scientific proof." The John Templeton Foundation of Radnor, Pennsylvania is funding rigorous neurobiological research on some elusive values such as love, meaning, creativity, mystical experience and curiosity. Larry

Dossey, MD author of *Healing Words: The Power of Prayer and the Practice of Medicine*, talks about how prayer studies on seeds have shown that the seeds that were prayed for did far better than the ones that were not. It didn't matter how far away they were, or if they were behind a lead shield. The scientific community is proving what the religions have told us all along. It is so exciting to see the spirituality and business conferences. Richard Barrett, former Values Coordinator at World Bank, has written *Liberating the Corporate Soul*. We are becoming whole again.

Whatever you want to call it – L energy, intimacy, caring, service, gratitude, prayer, values - well-being is about connecting with the Divine Force, opening our hearts and letting the Love flow.

 HERE'S ONE THOUGHT: I will remember a loving encounter and feel it fully before I decide what to say or do.

He HADN'T stopped U-Ville from singing! It sung! For down deep in the hearts of the old and the young, those Twin Towers were standing, called Hope and called Pride, And you can't smash the towers we hold deep inside. Unknown

MAKING CONTACT

September 11, 2001.

Most people remember where they were that morning and what they were doing when they heard.

I was in Orlando speaking at a national nurse manager convention. My session time was 8-9 AM. Since outside events were not known to us, we had a great time. I was talking with a participant following my presentation, when a woman walked up and asked us, "Did you hear what happened?" I wondered why she would interrupt our conversation to tell us a bit of news.

We could not have imagined what was happening as activity began all around us. Televisions were rolled out and set up in the convention hall corridors with chairs placed in front of them. You could feel something in the air.

We sat and we watched. No one said a word. We were mesmerized and horrified as the morning unfolded with more and more human-inflicted disaster. We were shocked and sickened as the appalling images were repeatedly burned into our memories.

Nurses from the greater D.C. and New York areas wanted to go home to help, but they had the same problem many people had: No airlines were operating. One of the nurse supervisors from New York City told me, "I couldn't wait to get away from the pettiness and discord of my unit. And today... I can't wait to get back. I want to help them. They'll be working so hard. They're a great bunch of people." This situation served to show her what really was important.

It was a time when we were all too aware that we never know when a life will end. People called their families just to say, "I love you." September 11, 2001 reminded us of the essential.

On the one hand there were people inflicting suffering and yet, on the other, we watched and heard of heroic and kindly actions of people working to alleviate the suffering. We all know of the emergency workers who ran *into* the buildings. And there were small miracles of kindness happening all around. There were stories of store owners passing out athletic shoes to women in high heels, taxis in New York City didn't charge. The Disney hotel gave free rooms to guests with airplane tickets they couldn't use. Car rental companies allowed patrons to drive wherever they wanted with no mileage charge or drop-off fee.

My flight was for Wednesday. Not knowing how much longer it would be before I could fly, I started home Friday morning by bus. It was a long ride with dazed and preoccupied silences happening much of the time. Still everyone seemed to be more cohesive than one would normally expect of strangers traveling together. There were many conversations on the bus and at the rest stops. People seemed to share more and connect with one another.

Connections were made between people who normally never would have met. I heard of residents of one small town who cared for the passengers of one of the grounded airplanes. To thank their benefactors, the travelers on that flight started a scholarship fund.

People brought the gifts they had. Some students offered their music to the workers. They came to the rest centers and played their instruments. They found people enjoyed what they offered just as it was, and did not judge. One student said that although he didn't play perfectly, he found out he didn't need to. He offered what he had and it was appreciated by the recipients. It was "vibrational medicine."

Caring, giving, grace and...humor? Yes, humor. As people walked down from the Towers and were tired, someone lifted their spirits with the suggestion to count off like New Year's Eve, 10, 9, 8, 7... and they were heartened as they called out the numbers and descended the last floors of the building. Humor was used as a way to have mental power over what could not be controlled.

Because keynote speakers couldn't fly in, I was invited to help close the conference with Dr. Judith Briles. She asked me to do a guided visualization. For the finale, Dr. Briles found a participant who could sing and invited her to close the conference with a song. The unaccompanied solo voice began singing *Amazing Grace.* She was joined by another voice. Then more and more voices rose as the conference attendees started standing, joined hands or arms and sang.

This appeared to be a time when it might seem strange to sing. Yet, this was a situation when we needed to raise our hearts and our voices. This was a period when objections to "God blessing" us weren't heard.

We reached down, we reached up, we reached out, we reached in, and ... we made contact with more than ourselves.

Each experience offers us the opportunity to gain knowledge and wisdom and increase in love and understanding. If there is a difficulty in your life, maybe there is something you can learn from it. No matter how devastating things appear, reach down, reach up, reach out, and reach in, because the most important of all is... to make contact. God bless us, everyone!

 HERE'S ONE THOUGHT: I am grateful for the others in my life.

Forgiveness is an inner correction that lightens the heart. It is for our peace of mind first. Being at peace, we will now have peace to give to others, and this is the most permanent and valuable gift we can possibly give. Forgiveness is a gentle refusal to defend ourselves against love any longer. Gerald Jampolsky

HERE COMES THE JUDGE

Have you ever been called to jury duty? How did you feel about that responsibility entrusted to you? Can you imagine having to judge before the case was presented? Could you render your verdict prior to hearing the evidence? Does that sound reasonable to you?

How about outside of the courthouse? At work, at home, at school? Have you ever judged, condemned and sentenced others without a fair trial? Is jumping to conclusions your exercise of choice?

Many of us are busy judging before all the evidence is in. There are parts and pieces of the whole truth that are not included when we find others "guilty." Even when we have all the evidence, we need to look beyond what is before us. We need to see with spiritual eyes to get the whole picture. And when we do that, the picture just may not look the same.

We can each only bear what we can bear. We have no idea what we would be like, if we lived another's life. Some people have quicker calls to anger. But most of us have our limits and get angry at some point. We may judge those who are quick to anger harshly. But if we ever get angry when we didn't want to, doesn't it become harder for us to judge others for the same thing just because they get there sooner? Why didn't we stop?

Some people are outwardly angry. Some people don't look angry but are passive aggressive. Is that better? If we honestly look within, we may see something we wish were not there. But wishing things are not there when they are, is an exercise in futility. We have to love and accept "*what is*," about others and about ourselves. What is the other option?

After one of my presentations on forgiveness, a woman came up to me and explained why she couldn't accept her divorce, why her ex-husband was wrong, and why he should be punished. By the way, he was already remarried and had been for years. So I said, "OK, you can accept it or....(long pause)...remind me (quizzical look), what was the other option?" Silence.

Pause. Small smile. "Or I could be bitter and miserable."

"Ahhh, yes, that's right, you can accept it OR you can be miserable. As long as you know it's your choice. And remember, the caustic chemical changes that occur in your body when you choose the second option. That punishes you not him."

We have to love and accept everyone for who he is because, after all, that is "what iz." However, we usually have a choice as to how we want to include them in our lives. We definitely have a choice as to where we focus our thoughts and which ones we choose to hold. Some thoughts may come unbidden, but the ones we contemplate are our choice. Viktor Frankl, the Austrian psychiatrist who was a prisoner in the Nazi camps, said, "the last of the human freedoms is to choose our own attitude." He called the thought patterns of some of the prisoners *Attitudinal Heroism.* What would he say about your patterns of thought? When you are contemplating non-judgment, consider carrying it over to yourself as well. Accept others and yourself, drop your judgments, focus on the blessings, don't condemn or sentence, contemplate the good, you'll feel better. Ha! It's just a selfish thing to do! ;-)

 HERE'S ONE THOUGHT: I'm dropping my judgments toward others AND myself.

To give dignity to a man is above all things. Native American Prayer

REACH BENEATH THE FLESH

There are so many people today talking about unity and diversity. It's become a "hot topic." Diversity can be celebrated and yet I think it's just a surface issue. As soon as you go deeper, you can see the oneness as in one body but many cells. I don't see unity as sameness at all – I see it about harmony, connection and cooperation.

Diversity is an exterior viewpoint. As soon as we get to know someone, up close and personal, looking more deeply, the differences disappear. I remember my sister once telling my father his bow tie didn't match his sports jacket. He told her, "When people are close enough to see this small tie, they won't notice the coat!"

Instead of focusing on the outside, we could build relationships. In today's multi-cultural and multi-racial society, it's sometimes difficult to know what the "PC" or politically correct action should be. I think if we are attempting to learn about the other person, if we are offering dignity and respect, then that message is felt. I believe there's a lot of information that passes between us that goes beyond words. If we can hold firm to our intention to be loving, others will feel that power.

There is wisdom in delighting in our differences, celebrating our gifts *and* realizing how much we are alike. I makes me feel better when I remind myself, just like me they've known pain, just like me they want love, just like me they want to be

96

happy. Our diversity shows us the abundance of the universe. Which is prettier, the lily or the rose? Which is more important, the brain or the heart? We want them all.

I heard a story about contact that was made between those who would usually avoid each other. They met at *Ground Zero.* One construction worker recounted his story. He went into the church to rest and noticed some green- and purple-haired kids with metal parts and pieces coming out of body areas he never knew one pierced. He admitted he normally wouldn't have had anything to do with them. But as he rested they came over to him and removed his burned shoes and wet socks. They rubbed his feet and put on dry socks and new boots. And he said, "I'll never look at them the same again." When we have a caring encounter, skin color, religion, nationality all fall away as we go beneath the flesh and meet soul to soul.

I remember meeting a woman who was talking about her small office. There were three people there. She claimed she was a big picture person, a real idea generator. She acknowledged she was blessed to have her staff, one who would pull her back, help her focus and tell her what they could afford to do and another who would get busy and do the work. If we can consciously celebrate the unique gifts and patterns and colors each person brings, we will discover that we are one harmonious design, a community of richness and strength.

What do you think would happen if you were willing to risk a situation that is outside your comfort zone and stay grounded in love? Who knows, maybe we can start another vicious cycle...a cycle of caring.

I challenge you to expand your thoughts:
To dream – What could my world look like?
To think – What can *I* do to make a difference?

To act – Am I living my life so that if everyone else followed my lead we would see heaven on earth?

 HERE'S ONE THOUGHT: How are others like me and what do they bring that's unique?

When I told a friend that I was doing a program on Diversity, it reminded her of a poem she wrote. I think it speaks well to the topic. It's called *Depth* and was written in 1968 when she was a teen.

> *Depth*
> *Look into, not at,*
>   *your fellow human being.*
> *Appearances but hide*
>   *what you could be seeing.*
> *Listen with your heart*
>   *for spoken words deceive.*
> *Feel not with your hand*
>   *and doing so - perceive.*
> *Take not but a part*
>   *of what is truly whole.*
> *Reach beneath the flesh*
>   *and touch the hidden soul.*
>   *Jane Milotte*

True unity and love is only possible when we connect with the soul. Materialism divides. Spirituality unites. The physical – the corporeal – is inherently divisive. Everything material occupies its space (and time), and thus precludes another from occupying its space. If you give some of your material possessions to another, you have less quantitatively. Qualitatively – spiritually – you however become wealthier. Spirit unites. Two people can occupy different spaces but their soul, which transcends space (and time) unites them as one. Rabbi Simon Jacobson

TEACHERS LIKE STUDENTS?

I have done school faculty/staff days or programs, and what I find interesting is that some teachers do what they wouldn't accept from their students.

At one school program, I was in the middle of a story, with the group fully engaged in listening. A teacher walked in very late, sat down and started talking to the person next to her who appeared annoyed by this distraction, not wanting to miss the end of the story. During a one-day workshop I've had participants tell me they lost their papers. They didn't even go anywhere between sessions. I had some questions for them to answer, and I invited the able-bodied to go outside for a "mindfulness walk." Some did not complete these simple assignments.

Note the choices that they made. Were they different from the actions and choices of their own students? There are things students don't want to do. Things they refuse to do. Sometimes papers get lost, some students don't show up, communication to friends can't wait. How similar are their choices? Are the adults like the children, or are the children like the adults?

More fodder for my theory that diversity is just a surface issue. Even in the age category, going deeper we find we are more alike than different.

One teacher described junior-high students as little kids in bigger bodies. The older I get, the more I see that we are all children, even those in aging bodies. I clipped a picture one day of a little girl. Her feet were half the size of the high heels she was standing in, and she was swimming in a fancy dress that was dragging on the floor. Perched on her head was a huge, broad-brimmed hat. I thought of a quote I had seen: "A grandma is just an antique little girl."

If someone knocked your glasses off your face and they landed on the floor, would you be angry? What if it was your new grandchild's jerky hand movements? Do you fly into a rage toward the baby? No, you take responsibility. It was you who got too close with the glasses. You didn't grab them in time. What if you considered some people as baby souls? What if they really didn't understand what they were doing? What if they haven't developed enough to do things well? What if someone pushed you in the grocery line, would that bother you? What if you turned and found an elderly woman had lost her balance and pushed you, as she fell to the floor?

I believe some people don't know what they're doing and some others can't seem to help themselves. Do you want to give them power to make you angry?

What if individuals are at different places or different ages of soul? If two travelers are going to California and one driver is in Pennsylvania and one is in Nevada, is one a better person? Just as we have to take into account chronological age, maybe we need to take into account spiritual age as well.

Consider this one: what if they're spiritually advanced and they have come back to help us. What if it was their job to push our buttons to challenge us to love better? Pause for a moment to ponder that thought!

No matter the reason they are in your life, how does this thought resonate with you? "Their words and behavior do not rule me. I will think, and speak, and act as I decide."

How do you want to live?

 HERE'S ONE THOUGHT: What if this person is a baby soul, or what if they are an enlightened being who is in my life to help me love better, even when it's hard?

Forgiveness is the key that unlocks the door of resentment and the handcuffs of hate. It is a power that breaks the chains of bitterness and the shackles of selfishness. William Arthur Ward

TRIGGER POINT THERAPISTS

When considering ourselves holistically, in terms of our mind, body and spirit, many people have integrated exercise into their lives as a method of balance. Have you considered bodywork, such as massage or trigger point therapy? Ayurvedic medicine recommends we give ourselves a daily massage because it helps drain the lymph nodes. The lymphatic system doesn't have a pump like the circulatory system, so contracting muscles through exercise or using hand pressure helps move the flow.

Some people consider massage too expensive, but you can do it for yourself, that's free. Aren't you worth $10 or $15 a week? What about $5? Just put the money aside and when you have enough, treat yourself to a massage. As with any profession, there will be individuals within it who are better than others. Get a recommendation and, even at that, what some people like may not meet the next person's needs. So if one doesn't work well for you, try another.

I went to a Zen therapist for a trigger point session. Trigger point therapy presses on a knotted muscle until it gives up. It lets go and releases. Interestingly enough, when the muscles are too tight, it feels like the therapist is hurting you.

I told him, "You're hurting me."

He said, "No, I'm not."

I said, "Yes, you are. I can feel it."

Again he said, "No. I'm helping to heal you."

Really?

When he was pressing on one particular "button," I arched my back to get away from his finger. It didn't help ease the pain. But when I let my body relax to its natural position, which happened to be *into* his finger, I began to feel better. How can moving into the painful pressure cause it to disperse?

Life is full of paradoxes.

What if you were to look at the people who push your emotional buttons as your therapists? What if they *are* healers – pointing out our problem spots and pushing until we let them go? What if it were true? Now that would give us cause to bless everyone in our lives.

What's so bad about that?

So now when you see a difficult person walking up to you, think: "Here comes my trigger point therapist!" The inside smile may even start the interaction off in a better way.

 HERE'S ONE THOUGHT: S/he's just my trigger point therapist, helping to heal me.

Forgiveness is a gentle refusal to defend ourselves against love any longer. Gerald Jampolsky

FORGIVE THEM? YOU'RE KIDDING?

Is it time to forgive someone? Maybe it's past time to forgive. But we can only do what we can do. Maybe something in this book will make a difference. And then... concerning the things you can't do, there is an exception..."I can do all things through God who strengthens me." Have you even asked for help?

Remember, forgiveness has nothing to do with the others, it's all about you. Forgiveness is about you, releasing your attachment to the pain. Stop embracing it. Let it go. It may be tying you down, or holding you back from moving on with joy. Release that rope of unforgiveness.

Sometimes we equate forgiveness with reconciliation. We refuse to forgive until....(fill in the blank). We bind it to someone saying they're sorry. We think forgiveness means there's no accountability. We can forgive and still hold someone responsible, like tough love. In deciding future actions, we hold no anger, but test each decision by asking: "What good would it do?"

I originally thought that old saying was a hopeless phrase, "Why bother, what good could it possibly do?" I don't see it that way anymore. It's not a hopeless comment. It's a touchstone. It's a touchstone of good. "What *good* will come from this?" It's a question to ask yourself. If nothing good, then maybe it would be best not to do it. If something good, then maybe it's best to do it, even if it's hard. But whatever you do, do it with love, not with anger or revenge.

You've read that five minutes of remembered anger can depress your immune system for up to six hours. You don't even have to be in the situation, just recalling it. "Stewing" is an excellent word to describe what you're doing with your internal chemistry. Unfortunately, it's a caustic chemical stew. Looking at it that way, forgiveness helps you, not them. I wrote a little limerick to help you remember the importance of letting go:

> There once was a tale of this guy,
> Who stored his grudges sky high,
> He poured poison in a cup,
> And he drank it all up,
> And expected the *Others* to die.

If that isn't reason enough, how about forgiving as you want to be forgiven? My best guess is many readers have often repeated these words: "forgive us our trespasses as we forgive others." If we don't forgive, are we then not forgiven? I know I've done things that need forgiveness, I don't want that to happen to me.

We all make mistakes. Mis-*takes*, wouldn't it be nice if we could do "*take 2*" or 4 or take 356? Or maybe we do get all the "*takes*" we need when we miss the mark.

I can understand why some people have a problem with no accountability. Not responsible seems to support future acts of the same kind. It's fine to have a consequence to help mold behavior. I think it's best that there be some lesson grounded in love. If I were the parent, I would want my child to have some kind of natural or reasonable consequence or there might be further trouble. Coming from a loving, not punitive place, is beneficial for everyone, including society. It would be best to have an outcome that will help perpetrators to see that there are ramifications to their actions that affect them too, since sometimes it appears they don't care about others.

Sometimes when you are not forgiving, you may be holding onto a judgment. That's something for you to look at long and hard. Sometimes wisdom calls us to dismiss the charges. Sometimes what needs to be forgiven is our own rash judgment.

You are CEO in your life. That stands for Co-creator, Experiencer and Opinion-maker. You decide whether you want to give others the authority over your peace of mind. If you make forgiveness contingent on their remorse, their saying "I'm sorry," their responding in some way, their doing *anything,* then you are giving your power to them. You give them control over when or *IF* you return from anger to peace. Meanwhile they're out having a great time.

Forgiveness is about you. It's For-*giving* you the gift of peace in this moment... and the next ones. Take back your power, forgive them, it's just a selfish thing to do!

By the way, I don't buy that story about the discovery of a new disease called Irish Alzheimer's! The symptom: you forget everything but your grudges.

 HERE'S ONE THOUGHT: I'm letting go of this before I get a rope burn or a broken arm; I'm "for giving" me peace.

LIVING IN THE PLEASANT

*Happiness is a perfume you cannot pour on others
without getting a few drops on yourself.*

Ralph Waldo Emerson

We've talked about living in the present, how about living in the pLeasant? Medical studies are being done to prove what some have already known – laugher is good for us. This is not new news. The Bible has told us a merry heart is good medicine (cheap too). Plato said, "Life must be lived as play." We now have the medical research that shows humor is a way to get our body as involved as possible in our healing processes. Author Deepak Chopra, MD has said, "Seriousness is equated with responsibility, when, in fact, I think we would be much more responsible if we had more joy and laughter in our lives." I do too.

Professor Lee Berk and Dr. William Fry at Loma Linda University in California have shown that mirthful laughter produces a physiological state comparable to that which follows vigorous exercise, reduces feeling of anger and aggressive behavior and positively affects immune functioning as well as being a beneficial cognitive coping mechanism. Other research shows that memory and learning are improved, stress hormones are down and emotional stability increases.

Joy and laughter is good for business too. It is only logical that when immune functioning is boosted, absenteeism and medical claims will be lower. With reduction of anger and aggressive behavior, communications and relationships will improve, teams will function better and morale will be higher. When you are having fun, you are more creative, energized and less accidents occur. Corporations, like Southwest Airlines, are finding that adding Love and Fun into their corporate character has added to their business success. They believe that the business of business is to make a profit by serving people and making life more fun. At Southwest Airlines, recruiting and hiring practices are built on the basis that humor helps.

Dr. Patt Schwab, author of *Leave a Mark, Not a Stain!*, states: there are 3 ways to motivate people to work harder, faster and smarter: 1. Threaten them. 2. Pay them lots of money. 3. Make their work fun. She contends "the first two have had a limited and short-term success rate. Only number three has a track record of effecting real change. It is time managers acknowledge humor as an interpersonal skill, and learn how to create an atmosphere that is challenging, creative and fun for employees as well as for themselves.

All over the country people are talking and infusing joy and laughter wherever they can. Allen Klein is a San Francisco based "jollytologist" and editor of the *Whole Mirth Catalog* and *The Healing Power of Humor*. When his wife was dying with cancer, he found the power in humor, even if only for a moment, which made the troubles easier to bear. He says, "It was like a mini-vacation that allowed us to regain our strength and pull our resources together." Circumstances may not change, but humor can give a feeling of power in situations where you felt you had none.

You don't even need to be exposed to something funny, you can just laugh. Yogic laughter with Dr. Madan Kataria is the doorway to joy for thousands of people in India and more converts around the world. He was inspired by Norman Cousins book *Anatomy of an Illness* that tells of the author's use of laughter as therapy and the extraordinary triumph over his "incurable" illness. Steve Wilson, Cheerman of the Bored and Karyn Buxman, RN can help you become a laughter leader with their World Laughter Tour. Or check out Joel Goodman and Margie Ingram of the Humor Project.

Joy has entered hospitals with the Clown Care Unit at NY City Presbyterian Hospital and Minnesota consultant Kristin Anderson told me that several of her hospital clients have created a "Humor Corner." In this space, employees (and even some patients and family members) clip and post cartoons and quotations. There is a basket of stress relieving toys and some comedy videos. Having a bad or stressful day? A coworker can "send you to the corner." Dr. Pat Raymond, a Virginia gastroenterologist knows the importance of a dose of fun. She shares her colonoscopy jokes and songs hoping to laugh fears away.

Even lawyers who leave you laughing? Attorney and humorist Jeff Fleming, from Illinois uses humor to relax his clients in the office. Many times when they see him they are going through a difficult time. It may be a death or dissolution of a marriage. Fleming contends, "if we can raise their humor level, it helps them to cope, even if it the circumstances remain the same."

We know that our mood affects our body. Did you know that your body affects your mood as well? Western culture hasn't yet come to understand that mind and body are not separate, but you don't have to believe me. Just test it in your life. The next time you feel down, choose to smile and skip, wave your arms in the air and sing or shout "Yippee!" Do you feel depressed when you are doing that? You might feel foolish, but I doubt depressed.

Skipping is a powerful message of joy to your body. Running could be from a fearful situation, but skipping is connected to a childhood feeling of glee. If you're embarrassed to do it alone, find a young child to join you. That can give you a good excuse (if you need one).

You can smile and laugh for no reason. Thich Naht Hahn a Vietnamese monk recommends taking a deep breath and smiling whenever you hear a bell. You can breathe and smile whenever you start the car, come to a traffic light, or before you pick up the phone. Smiles not only work their way out, they also can work their way in. Mother Teresa recommended to people to "smile more, smile at those you love, and smile at strangers."

When you're happy, you smile; that's a pretty traditional thought. But did you know it works the other way too? The physical act of smiling tells your body it's happy. Consider putting a pencil in your mouth sideways, with the points sticking out the sides. Then push it in, as far back as far as possible and voila – a smile. I call that a #2 smile! (#3 pencils and pens also work! ;-)

Practice makes improvement. Remember humor boosts immunity, and reduces levels of classic stress hormones and the damage they may cause. Also, following laughter you experience the relaxation response. You can read funny stories or jokes, and share them. When you socialize consider playing games that make you laugh. Choose to be with people who make you laugh. Use props that make you laugh. Look for the humor everywhere including, maybe especially, in mistakes and imperfection.

Not only is there safe stress, there is safe humor. Be sure the humor is kind and gentle and fun for everyone. Sarcasm means rip or tear and ridicule is cruel. Drop the put downs. The safe humor test asks, "Does it lift people up? Does it bring people closer? Is it based on caring and empathy?"

Learn to laugh at yourself, you'll have a constant supply of good material! When you look from a new perspective, you may find the humor-being. Consciously choose to bring more laughter into your life. When you are joy for others, you can't keep it from yourself.

111

Living in the pleasant and helping others get there is a great combination. Adopt an attitude of raising spirits—one that allows individuals to escape or thrive during loss and change, encourages risk taking, supports staying creative under pressure and nourishes good health – that's the way to the well-being of individuals, teams, families and organizations.

Bring on the cheer-leaders! Let's have more fun and laughter in our lives. It's good for our bodies, it will lift our spirits and...the bottom line.

 HERE'S ONE THOUGHT: This situation calls for a #2 smile!

Be more Stress Hardy – Develop your humor habits:
-Start the day laughing for no reason
-Read funny stories or jokes – share them
-Play games that make you laugh
-Be with people who make you laugh
-Appreciate absurdities
-Use props that make you laugh
-Create a humor corner – then use "go to the corner"
-Look for the humor everywhere (including, maybe especially, in mistakes and imperfection)
-Think it will be funny later? Then think it's funny now you'll have much more fun.
-Laugh at yourself (never cease to be amused)
-Smile more, they work their way in
-#2 smile = pencil sideways in mouth, push way back (#3 led pencils will also work :-)
-Look from a new perspective or angle
-Consciously choose to bring more laughter in your life.
-Keep a playful attitude

-Be joy for others, you can't keep it from yourself.
Why Humor? Jest because.

Learn to laugh; it is a discipline to be mastered. Let go of the everlasting burden of always needing to sound profound. Richard Foster

GETTING HIGH SMILEAGE

When talking to groups about humor I will ask if anyone has a story they want to share. And I'll ask you too - if you have a tale that's funny or a thought that helped you, please let me know about it. In one of my seminars, a woman shared a story about a day she was on a bus trip. She explained that it was a big bus, the kind with the bathroom in the back. She needed to use the bathroom but she didn't want to get up and walk back there, because if she did... everyone would know... what she wanted to do!

Finally, she was too uncomfortable so she risked it, walked to the back and tucked herself into that tiny space.

She told us, "I had to pull my pants way down. Then... the bus swerved. I lost my balance and fell against the door. It opened and... I fell out. The bus swerved back and I fell back in. Then... I didn't want to get out for the rest of the trip!" Everyone in the seminar burst into gales of laughter.

I thought it was interesting that this woman who was embarrassed to let anyone on the bus know that she had normal bodily functions was now standing up before 250 people sharing her story about the day she fell out of the bathroom on the bus with her pants down.

Time does give us a new perspective.

Often it's the embarrassing moments of our lives that bring joy to ourselves and others in the retelling. We find it easy to laugh when it happens to someone else. Why not grab that laugh even when it happens to you?

I wish you 40 SPG!

SPG = Smiles to the gallon.

HERE'S ONE THOUGHT: This would be funny if it happened to someone else; I may as well get all the smileage I can out of this event, even if it's happening to me.

To be wealthy, a rich nature is the first requisite and money but the second. To be of a quick and healthy blood, to share in all honorable curiosities, to be rich in admiration and free from envy, to rejoice greatly in the good of others, to love with such generosity of heart that your love is still a dear possession in absence or unkindness -- these are the gifts of fortune which money cannot buy, and without which money can buy nothing.
Robert Louis Stevenson

WHAT'S IN YOUR SAVORINGS ACCOUNT?

I taught a three credit distance-learning class on Wellness and had students from all over the United States taking part. One of the assignments asked them to write about three intensely happy memories. The descriptions were rich, the images vivid and the feelings usually so well expressed that the joy was palpable, fairly bubbling off the papers.

I invited the students to keep these assignments. Then, when their spirits needed a lift, they could review their words, recall those moments and touch those happy feelings again.

Have you saved your special cards or recorded somewhere the words or actions that were points of light to you? Consider doing such a thing personally, as a family or as an organization.

Participants in my course did a lot of soul searching. They became conscious of how they were moving through their lives and how that compared with the vision of what they wanted for their life. Only when you've examined both can you know where adjustments need to be made to bring the two into alignment.

How often have you considered your existence, how you live and what your heart desires? Do you write your large goals and the smaller steps to get there, and keep the vision before you at work and at home? Do you celebrate your successes and remember and give thanks for all the kindnesses there have been in your life?

Each time you move toward your vision, and each time you bathe in gratitude, you change your body chemistry, your heart variability pattern and the family, organization, school or community climate.

You are a beacon. You can choose to emanate satisfaction and thankfulness or anxiety and anger. Either way, it's up to you, and it's contagious to others who are also broadcasting around you.

Here's the secret! You go first.

How much do you have in your life savorings account? It's more important than money.

 HERE'S ONE THOUGHT: Let me review what I have in, and find more things to add to my savorings account.

Laugh at yourself and at life. Not in the spirit of derision or whining self-pity, but as a remedy, a miracle drug, that will ease your pain, cure your depression, and help you to put in perspective that seemingly terrible defeat and worry with laughter at your predicaments, thus freeing your mind to think clearly toward the solution that is certain to come. Og Mandino

BORROWING FUTURE LAUGHTER
MULTIPLIES FUN

I am sure you can relate to something in your past that wasn't so funny at the time. But now, as you retell the story, it brings laughter and joy. So, what's the difference? Distance and perspective? If we can take the "witness" view in this moment, maybe we can enjoy it better now.

My middle son had a college composition course that assigned a task to write about the worst day in his high school career. He titled it: "What Is That Smell?" It was about a day when he left his clothes in the washing machine too long, and, to quote him, "They'd begun to go bad." This didn't cause him but a moment's hesitation because according to Tyler, "Everyone knows when clothes come out of the dryer, they're warm, fluffy and smell good."

That fall morning Tyler learned that this is not always the case. But he went on to hope: "Perhaps through some strange twist of dryer magic my shirt would have escaped the smell."

No such luck.

As a heavy-set freshman, he wrote "I raced upstairs as fast as my rotund little legs could carry me to look for another olfactory opinion." Tyler proceeded to describe how I took his sleeve and held it up near my nose. He said I made a terrible face and told him, "It's not that bad........unless you get real close," which seemed to appease him.

He did wear the shirt. He says, "Just like every other day I went to my locker and put my books away, and just like every other day I went to the cafeteria to sit with new friends, and that's where the "just like every other day" came to an abrupt halt." This was Tyler's first year in a new school. He was sitting with some students he didn't know very well and one of them asked, "What is that smell?" Tyler looked toward the kitchen, "I don't know what they're having for lunch today but I'm not having any."

It was immediately following the question, "What's that stuff they keep fetal pigs in?" that Tyler turned red and beat a hasty retreat. He met a friend in the hall and told him to be quiet and asked how bad the smell was. "Oh no," he yelled, "You reek!"

"I have never looked forward to the bell sounding the end of the day more than on that day, when I decided to wear my smelly shirt. Every minute seemed like an eternity. I knew people on the other side of the room were grimacing due to my pungency. The teachers seemed to teach more to the other side of the room. Whenever their pacing brought them to within a few feet of my stench, they began walking in a different direction."

Somehow I feel this might be an exaggeration. I do know that it was painful for him that day, and he has had and shared much joy with his story since then. Tyler read his composition to some neighbors who were crying tears of laughter before he finished.

How many times have you laughed at your foibles when you've had the courage to share them? Time and grace transform our pain and sorrow. The gift will come when you can take that step back in the moment, rise above and look down at yourself.

 HERE'S ONE THOUGHT: Will this be funny later? Then if I can see it's funny now, I'll have much more fun!

The amount you laugh in your relationships with others is the true measure of the health of your personality.
Brian Tracy

ROAD RAGE OR ROAD ROARS

My sister and I used to take a vacation at the start of every summer with our mother. Memory makers are a great idea. We've had wonderful laughs and times to remember so we can laugh again. My sister is a great storyteller about all that happens. She tells of the trip north from Connecticut to New Hampshire to meet me with Mom in her car. She was looking for a particular route number. As she was driving, she requested help from Mom to look for Route 239. I am not at liberty to discuss her age at the time, but Mom had been a senior citizen for some time. She was active and vital, volunteering at a local hospital, playing bridge and driving herself to those places, very much on the ball. But with red hair and the story I'm about to tell, you might think she was more like Lucille Ball.

As they were driving down the road, my mother had taken on her navigation task with great seriousness, eyes pealed, and she finds 239 almost as they pass it, but warns my sister, "Quick, there it is, 239!" My sister begins to turn but she couldn't find the road. She decided to turn in to a service station to get her bearings. The sign my mom had spied was $2.39, the gas price!

They laughed then, I laughed when I heard the tale, and others have laughed at the retelling.

That story reminds me of another car adventure, traveling to an evening meeting with two friends (I'll call them Jane and Joe to protect the guilty!) We found ourselves driving around unable to locate the building we needed. It was mostly a residential area with some closed businesses when Joe points and exclaims, "Look! Domino's Pizza is open!"

I was glad to know he didn't fit the stereotype of a man unwilling to ask for directions.

His next words were, "We can order a pizza!"

I'm thinking I should have guessed. He's tall and thin and always hungry. Sometimes he's brought a snack.

Then he proceeds to divulge the complete plan. It was to order the pizza, have it delivered to our planned destination and follow the driver there.

We howled.

In sharing both those stories with a friend, she told me it wouldn't have been funny for her, not then and not later. She related that her husband would have been angry and he would have belittled her. It would have been misery for her. And he was making misery for himself. What a shame to do that to the same incidents that have brought so much joy.

When you look at life, how do you see it? Which way do you choose? When you might be tempted to make simple things too complex and serious, you are invited to look for the humor, give thanks and a mighty roar of laughter.

 HERE'S ONE THOUGHT: Let me look at this from the other side. How can I find the humor?

Take time to laugh. It is the music of the soul. Old Irish Prayer

THE FUN ANGLE

I've mentioned before, "If you think this might be funny later, think it's funny now and have way more fun." In doing so, I hear some great stories, experiences that people didn't enjoy so much in the moment, but time has gifted them with a new perspective – the fun angle.

I had broken my arm and was at the physical therapist's office doing some exercises that hurt. Because I know that laughter can help ease pain, I asked my therapist Kate if she had any funny stories to share. She proceeded to tell me about a day when she was walking in a large discount store and felt something dragging by her foot. Do your thoughts immediately go to toilet tissue? At our speaker conferences, many have mentioned that particular predicament, unfortunately noticing too late, as they walked across the main stage, with the errant product following along attached to their shoe.

No, it wasn't toilet tissue. When she looked down she saw, to her horror, it was... a pair of her underpants! That's right. Her underwear was becoming outerwear at the bottom of her right pant leg.

As quickly, smoothly and cleverly as possible, she swooped down, picked them up and stuffed them into her pocket. She told me she didn't look at anyone so that no one could see her. That was an interesting bit of information and a

123

good stress tip I thought. I didn't realize that if you don't look at someone, you can't be seen. This is an important piece of information for me; I could have used it in any number of circumstances!

Looking on the bright side, she gave thanks her rogue underwear was clean. Apparently the static of the dryer held them in the pant leg, but they worked their way down later as she walked, poking out at the worst opportunity.

I thought it was funny, but wait... When she told someone else, their immediate question was: "How did it get off the other leg?" We laughed again.

Considering gratitude, yes, she was thankful they were clean. Another person pointed out something else to be grateful for – she could give thanks that she wasn't caught and arrested for shoplifting!

With the laughter the pain was reduced and I did manage to get more exercising in that day too.

I remember singing a hymn that had the words "the sacrifice of joy." It made me wonder what kind of a sacrifice joy could possibly be? And then I saw it this way. Sometimes we don't feel like being joyful. I believe that in being fully alive to all God has given us we have to honor all of life's gifts, even the gift of sorrow. And sometimes we can shift to bring joy to our world, even when we don't feel like it – a sacrifice of joy: to love and lift those others we find in our lives.

Mother Teresa said, "Joy is love, the normal result of a heart burning with love. Joy is a need and a physical power. Our lamp will be burning with sacrifices made out of love if we have joy."

If you need a gift idea for yourself, maybe you could get a *perspectoscope* and use it to help you focus in on the fun angle.

HERE'S ONE THOUGHT: If joy is a need and a physical power, help me find the fun-angle in this circumstance.

Lynn Durham

LETTING GO

The basic lesson is letting go.
When I am getting burned I let go.
Amazing, the inner peace that comes from
separation from wrong things.
John MacNulty

In the physiology of stress, hormones are released into our blood stream. The blood pressure and pulse go up. You've probably felt it before. The respiratory rate goes up. It's rapid but it's shallow moving air in and out of the upper airways where no oxygenation takes place. That's why a deep diaphragmatic breath is so important. It pulls the oxygen down into the alveoli, the tiny air sacks where the exchange with carbon dioxide occurs. Blood is shifted away from the gastrointestinal tract to the large muscles. That would be good in case you need to run but not good if you need to digest. This cascade of events is referred to as fight or flight. We are on the ready to attack or run.

And yes, the platelets get sticky, which is beautiful body wisdom if we are running from a saber toothed tiger and might get mauled. We would be ready to clot faster and stem the bleeding. But making our platelets sticky when we're stuck in traffic is not a good plan, especially if our coronary arteries are restricted. It might get us in trouble.

My guess is most of us haven't needed to run from tigers. Yet, all the physiological events are still occurring when we're stressed. By a change of our thoughts and feelings we can make a difference in our body. Consider carefully what you are choosing for yourself.

I knew a man who had elevated blood pressure and was in constant pain from arthritis which restricted his usual activities. When he left a bad relationship, the arthritis went away and his blood pressure returned to normal. What was going on? Is it possible he let go of some of his anger?

Maybe it's not a person but some other attachment that would serve us best if it were released.

I spoke at a conference in Pennsylvania. Afterwards I received copies of the evaluations. One participant commented that the loud music in the adjacent room was somewhat distracting "...but it wasn't worth sticky platelets."

I do a short guided visualization with a lemon. After audience members share that they noticed how they salivated, I ask, "Why would that be?" There was no lemon to see or touch or smell, yet chemical changes were occurring throughout the body-mind. Our thoughts are not separate from the body.

For a good laugh search www.youtube.com for Bob Newhart - stop it. How many times are we unwilling to let go of the thoughts that are causing us pain.

Sometimes it's important to hold on and sometimes the greater wisdom comes in letting go.

 HERE'S ONE THOUGHT: Is this worth sticky platelets?

No matter how outrageous or unfair others might appear to you, they do not, never did, and never will upset you. The bitter truth is that you're the one who's creating every last ounce of the outrage you experience.
David Burns, MD

FROM ANGER TO PEACE

Did you read that quote? Ouch, I'm creating my own outrage?

Yes, we are, by the thoughts that we hold.

Thoughts may come to you unbidden but you get to choose which thoughts you let pass by and which thoughts you choose to hold. I hope you choose peaceful thoughts. Would you accept things just the way they are (because after all, they are that way)? When?

We are expert players of the "Blame Game." But I am challenging you to take back your power. Stop giving your power away to others; stop maintaining your victim role. It doesn't matter what's going on around you, you are the one creating a caustic stew or chicken soup in your body by the thoughts you entertain. Entertain is a good word. You receive these thoughts as guests; you feed them, support them and keep them. Wouldn't it be better to be careful "who" you invite? And which thoughts you choose to "keep?"

The Institute of HeartMath in California has studied anger using salivary IgA (immunoglobulin A). "What this study showed is that even a single episode of recalling an experience of anger and frustration can depress your immune system for almost an entire day." Your thoughts affect what happens in your body.

I remember driving my son to school one morning. We were late; he was frustrated and angry. I reminded him that he could choose to ride to school angry, OR he could change his attitude (and body chemicals) and we could visit and enjoy the ride. Either way, he was late. It's not always easy, I have to practice again and again to reach what I preach.

When a car cuts you off, do you get angry? One of my games is to make up what might be going on for them.

A friend's son was attacked by a dog, and his dad was rushing him to the hospital. He passed a car on the right, on a curve where the car actually had its right wheels up a small incline. His son was bleeding next to him in the car. It was an emergency. I wonder about the driver of the car he passed. Was he angry or upset at this father's attempt to help his child?

Now when a car passes you in traffic, you can be angry at that "jerk" or you can choose to think that it might be an emergency. Maybe a loved one is dying at the hospital. Maybe not, who knows, but ask: "What serves *me* best?"

I'm not asking you to condone every action. You can work toward creating change, but what has already happened has already happened. The point is: "What now?" More specifically: "What am *I* going to do now?" Are you going to choose to be out of control, or are you going to respond with wisdom and effectiveness to what is going on around you? You decide.

You can use your anger, but don't abuse it. Peace Pilgrim put it well. She didn't ask that anger be suppressed; that wouldn't be good for us. Expressing our anger all over those near us isn't good for anyone involved either. Some people express their anger violently and then say they feel better. Besides the physiological changes, relationships are at risk of being destroyed, relationships which are the fabric of life. When people freely express their anger in unhealthy ways, they can create more heartache and problems for themselves, often resulting in marriage breakups or job losses. Peace Pilgrim said the best to deal with anger is to "confess it" not to suppress it.

Confessing it means being up front and explaining how you feel. If we can be real with our feelings and talk about our frustrations, miracles can happen. I call it my AIR it out method. Here's how it works:

- A - Use anger as an *Alarm*. We are put on notice that something is bothering us. We feel an injustice.
- I - Then it needs to be *Inspected*. Why does it bother us so? If we look at our anger bravely, we can usually discover a fear that needs to be faced.
- R – After we have used the anger for learning, then *Release* it. Let it go.

Looking for the fears is important. Have you been angry at a child because you didn't know where they were? It may have been because you were afraid something might have happened to them. Or if they didn't listen, are you afraid they will grow up not respecting you? What are you afraid of?

Many people have developed an anger "habit." Granted, it works in some cases to intimidate others into getting your way. Yet, it's also works against them, in alienating others, depressing their immune functioning and other negative physical reactions.

You're one thought away from feeling better. Next time you're angry, consider these thoughts:

This is just an alarm! What is my fear beneath it? What is my hope? I can choose peace in any moment. I am more effective when I am in control and feel better about it. It's better for me, and them, and the world.

You can do it. It just takes practice, repeating again and again your reach for relief.

 HERE'S ONE THOUGHT: Is there a fear here somewhere that bothers me so about this?

Life is either a daring adventure, or nothing. Security does not exist in nature, nor do the children of men as a whole experience it. Avoiding danger is no safer in the long run than exposure. Helen Keller

THE DIVAN

My mother had a couch – a good sturdy, extra-long couch. It was a little long for the wall where it sat when I was growing up, but my father was tall, so it was good to have a long couch so he could stretch out. Actually, Daddy didn't sit on the sofa. He had his "own" chair with an ottoman that he usually used. We children found it a good place for little treasure hunts under the seat cushion. Loose change would fall out of his pockets and wait for us there to discover it. (I've sometimes wondered if he put the coins in there. I don't notice change falling out of my pockets.)

After a while, my mother parted with the "divan" as she called it and bought a new couch that better fit the space. She gave the old one to her sister and there it lived for many years. When my aunt prepared to move to a nursing home, my mother paid to buy the couch at my aunt's yard sale. Yes, the same sofa she had given away years before. But, it was still in excellent condition with its expensive pink brocade fabric, and, besides, it was a good, sturdy, extra-long couch.

The problem now was where to put it. My mother didn't really need a couch; she already had enough furniture. So, it went on the porch temporarily. Even though there was no room for it on the porch. It lived there for over a year, enjoying the glassed-in porch. No one else could because it took up so much space in the middle.

I can remember the discussions between my sister and my mother. There was the quality of the couch versus my sister's wisdom that it wasn't needed and even worse, it was in the way. I think the reminder of my dad may have had some influence on the desire for my mom to keep it.

My sister even requested that I tell one of my sons to ask his grandmother if he could take it. Mom would be glad to give it to one of her grandsons for his house. My son told me he didn't want it. My sister's response was, "Tell him he won't have to take it far!" We all laughed. We shared the story with my mother and she laughed too.

It was difficult for Mom to let go. She finally managed to call the Salvation Army to pick up her old couch. She even got to use the porch for a few weeks in September of that year.

So many times what we are keeping gets in the way of better things for us.

What are you holding onto that no longer serves you?

 HERE'S ONE THOUGHT: I have enough. I am willing to let _____ go.

Success is the ability to go from one failure to another with no loss of enthusiasm. Sir Winston Churchill

RELEASING THE FEAR OF FAILURE

When my oldest son was in junior high school, we talked about bending over to touch your toes. I asked him to try. He barely leaned forward, his fingertips going down by his knees. "Brett, I mean really try." He said, "I am."

After doubting him once more (what a mom!), I discovered he was right. Boy, was he tight! We ended up going to the doctor who told him not to run or jump. His long bones had grown so fast that the tendons and ligaments hadn't kept up with them. We went to physical therapy three times a week for a while and he did exercises at home for years.

Then, as a sophomore in high school, Brett received the go ahead to get moving again. His friends had continued playing ball and had increased their skills. I remember a discussion I had with Brett. He wanted to try out for basketball but he was afraid he wouldn't make the team. I told him, the only thing he was guaranteed was, if he didn't try out, he wouldn't make the team. If he did try out, and the coach was smart, he would bring him on the team to have him practice every day. (Brett is now 6'7".)

The coach told him to come to practice. He would see if Brett tried hard and improved. So even though Brett wasn't sure he'd make the team, he gave it his all. When he came home from school with a uniform, I said, "Congratulations, you made the team!" He said no, Coach hadn't told him yet. When he prepared to go to the first game, I congratulated him again. He said no, he hadn't been told. I said, "Brett, you've made the team; he just forgot to tell you."

My son wanted to try out for the AAU (Amateur Athletic Union) team, but try-outs were across the state and none of his friends wanted to go. He went anyway, alone, and he made the team. Brett raised the money himself to travel to Arkansas for the final games.

From junior varsity he was moved up to varsity and then came the night that he wrote about it in his college application essay, "Believing in Yourself." He felt proud when they announced the starting center: "Brett *Buulllll* Durham."

His senior year was like the movie *Hoosiers.* He attended a high school that wasn't as big as the other class L (large) teams in the state. His team lost three of the first four games. Slated to come in 11th in the league, they worked really hard. With a great team effort and a little magic, they didn't lose again.

The night of the championship game, the bus had an escort out of town to the Interstate – all the emergency apparatus, lights and sirens. They were greeted the same way after the game when they pulled off I95 with the trophy. The townspeople were standing out in their yards waving as the bus and cars went by. The sign at the movie theater was changed to congratulate them and a restaurant reopened late to offer the team a steak or lobster dinner.

Brett went on to play four years of varsity basketball at RPI (Rensselaer Polytechnic Institute in Troy, NY). He was team captain for two years, and still holds records there in blocked shots and rebounds with his name on the wall. In his senior year, they made it all the way to the "Sweet Sixteen."

137

Imagine the excitement, awards and camaraderie Brett would have missed if he had been unwilling to risk the chance of failing to make the team.

Why do children think they have to do it well to try out? Do we as parents put too much pressure on them? Are all of us afraid to fail or to have others see us fail? What if it was okay to fail?

Maybe if we feel led to do something, we should just do it. Maybe it's okay if it doesn't work out. Maybe what we need to do is practice harder at whatever it is and try again. The main thing may be to just follow our hearts. The key being to listen, to hear what it's saying to us.

 HERE'S ONE THOUGHT: It's not failure, just practice. What do I feel led to do?

We attach our feelings to the moment when we were hurt, endowing it with immortality. And we let it assault us every time it comes to mind. It travels with us, sleeps with us, hovers over us while we make love, and broods over us while we die. Our hate does not even have the decency to die when those we hate die - for it is a parasite sucking OUR blood, not theirs. There is only one remedy for it. Forgiveness. Lewis Smedes

SHAME ON YOU

I was coaching a woman, Beth, who was mentioning an incident where she felt extremely uncomfortable. She was at the park with her grandson Jeremy. Beth and another parent started talking to each other. The other woman referred to Jeremy as her son. Beth told her, "He's my grandson." Amazed, the other lady said, "You look too young to be a grandmother!" Then, uncomfortable and embarrassed, Beth turned red. Apparently this was something that had bothered Beth for a long time.

Weeks later it came up that Beth had gotten pregnant as a teen. She had married the father only after her child was born. There was a swirl of emotion, shame and blame wrapped around them at that time. Neither knew why they married. Did they truly love each other or was it just because of the baby? Both felt pressured into the marriage because of the circumstances and family influence.

139

I asked her to think of a teenager she knew, maybe a niece or a neighbor. Then I asked, "If that child came to you and told you she was pregnant, would you forgive her?"

There was silence for a moment on the other end of the phone. I waited while that question was considered. Finally Beth spoke. She didn't say, "Yes, I would forgive her." Beth had gone beyond that to, "There's nothing to forgive about a baby."

And as we talked a little more about it, I heard the story of two teens in love. It sounded like they would have married anyway. They've had a good relationship for over 25 years, with four children and two grandchildren. Beth got a special gift for her husband to tell him that she would have chosen him anyway, and that she was glad she had married him. She was sorry she was hesitant at the time and hoped that he knew she was grateful that it had happened. She didn't know if she would have been able to otherwise commit and might have missed having all those years with this wonderful man and their great children. She told him how happy she was that she married him and would do it over again if she had the chance.

More than the embarrassment was changed. The relationship grew even stronger.

I shared that story with a friend in New Mexico. He thought it was powerful and asked if I had written it down. I said no. He encouraged me to share it because he felt there were many other people who could identify and who would in some way be affected, maybe even healed by it, as he felt he had been.

Issues, like having a messy office, could be as seemingly unimportant to some. For others, they hold a big charge. Would you forgive someone about a messy office? Moments before it had seemed overwhelming to him, now he laughed. There was nothing to forgive. And in the light of that insight the self-abuse and resultant paralysis seemed to dissolve. I think self-forgiveness may be the hardest of all.

Back to Beth in the park, I'm wondering, what's wrong with someone thinking a grandson was your baby? Is that bad? Isn't it better than the other way around? Like when that guy thought my youngest was my grandchild! ;-)

 HERE'S ONE THOUGHT: What would I think of a person if I heard them speak aloud to someone else what I just said to myself?

Since the perfect human being has not been discovered, we all need to live with our hang-ups and our idiosyncrasies until they can be ironed out. One of the most important qualities in successful, dynamic living is that of self-acceptance. Denis Waitley

WEAPONS OF MASS DISTRACTION

I know I want things to go "perfectly" and when they don't, it can be frustrating for me. Preferring perfection is one thing but attachment to it causes pain, AND the paradox is: It's all perfect. How you know it was "supposed" to go that way is – because it did.

It's difficult or embarrassing at times for me to admit my failings and foibles, and at the same time it's freeing. As I write this I'm thinking a stressful thought: "I hope they don't consider me stupid." That makes me feel terrible. And then a better thought, "What they think of me is none of my business." That makes me feel terrific.

So here I go, I have a story I'll risk sharing.

One day my car wouldn't start. I'd only had it a short time. Turning the key, it wouldn't even make a sound. I was frustrated, I was going to be late and I needed help.

A neighbor's son was kind enough to come over with a charger. He hooked it up to my battery, but nothing happened. He got his mom to drive over so we could jump-start it with her car battery. Still nothing. Men working across the street had pity on me and came over to help. They thought that no noise when the ignition is turned was a bad sign.

142

Then one man asked, "Is it in neutral?"

I used to have a standard transmission. Remember, I told you I'd only had the car a short time? Let me see what other excuses I can come up with! The sorry fact is I was the late for my appointment, I got everyone involved, and it was all because the car was in...Drive.

It seems like there should be a lesson here. Apparently I wasn't being mindful when I got out of the car, nor was I when I got back in it. I was in too much of a hurry. Where were my thoughts? I have no idea, probably all over the place. One of our weapons to keep us from peace is mass distraction.

I needed to slow down and center, and be in the moment fully. It helps if each time we get into our car and before we get out that we take a couple of deep breaths. That would be a good reminder to slow down and pay attention.

Another thing I've noticed is that when something is too hard, we're probably not doing it the right way. I was doing something wrong. Life isn't designed to be difficult. When we are going in the direction of our "flow," things are more enjoyable and come more easily.

Instead of thinking "How stupid am I?" I could go with, "I guess I needed some attention." I got it too!

Better yet, instead of *getting* attention, maybe slowing down and *paying* attention would be a better plan.

 HERE'S ONE THOUGHT: I am shifting into neutral, taking a deep breath and going more mindfully, choosing to give up feeling terrible and move to feeling terrific.

Lynn Durham

GET CREATIVE JUICES FLOWING

*When I examine myself and my methods of thought,
I come to the conclusion that the gift of fantasy
has meant more to me than my talent
for absorbing positive knowledge.*
Albert Einstein

For the health of yourself and your business it's good to be innovative, so let those creative juices flow.

Have you noticed what a natural high you get from creating? Just coming up with ideas that will make something easier or more profitable can make you feel good. "Possibility thinking" is energizing.

During one of my coaching sessions, my client was torn between two options. I challenged him: "What about G?" "OK," he said, and then asked me, "What does that mean?" I explained he was only looking at choices A and B. He hadn't even considered C, never mind D, E, F or G! When we are willing to seek other potential solutions, when we open our minds to the myriad of possibilities, ideas will come to us.

To have a successful idea session, don't judge your thoughts, merely receive them. Collect them all. Write them down. One idea may spark another. A funny one will add laughter, and following laughter you elicit the relaxation response, a physiological state opposite the stress response.

When participating in group brainstorming, do the same; welcome each suggestion. When a baby idea is presented and immediately put down or squelched by someone, it prevents future ideas from that person or others in the group who fear the same thing may happen to them. It can make the whole event unpleasant and unhealthy.

Some problems are more difficult and may call for an L, M or P. My theory is to go "Beyond Z." Come up with at least 27 ideas, one more than the 26 letters of the alphabet. I've quoted a lot of doctors... may as well use one called Seuss, for his inspiration of going beyond z in ideas instead of animals. If you had to come up with that many ideas each one would be greeted warmly. "Great, that's one less we have to go!" And in that acceptance and reception, it's easier for brains to bloom, generating more thoughts and dreams.

Someone once said, "Minds are like parachutes; both work best when open." Open your mind and help others to keep theirs open to the potential. Gather all the ideas, without judgment. Receive them with gratefulness. (Gratitude is good for your health! It changes your heart variability pattern. ;-) If you agree, it might be fun to charge a coin for each negative comment as a reminder to release judging. It's a way to raise awareness of the negativity so a new way can be chosen. Afterwards you can take the ideas you've been given and narrow them down to the best of the best, no condemnation necessary.

When presented with your next "problem," I invite you to rename it a "challenge" and plan to keep coming up with solutions...going beyond Z.

 HERE'S ONE THOUGHT: I want to rest in the solutions; is my mind open to possibility thinking?

Here is a poem I wrote to help you remember:

Problem Solving –
Rest in the Solutions:

When thinking solutions,
        how many do you see?
We normally think, A or B
        ...maybe C
Some people can make it
        even to D

How about going to
        E, F or G?
One problem may call for
        L, M or P
Some challenges urge to keep going
        to T
The creative can make it
        to U and to V
But the best of the thinkers go on...
        beyond Z!

Creativity is a learnable skill. It's not something that just happens to people. You can cultivate your own creativity, but it may require a shift in mindset. So often, people think creativity belongs to the known artists and inventors. They think it is a special talent. Creativity belongs to everyone. Willis Harmon

BEYOND Z

I use the Beyond Z method to help clients gather ideas for solutions to their problems. Here is a message I received back from a woman who gave it a try:

Thank you SOOO much for your wise counsel this morning. Your brilliant idea of doing the "BEYOND Z LIST" definitely worked in several ways. One, it enabled me to shift (as in "one thought away?") from feelings of fear and powerlessness and that sinking feeling that my entire world is out of control to feelings of competence, potential success, and the feeling that there are things I can do right now, today, to make a difference. I even got John's (admittedly reluctant) buy-in. He was hesitant to start, so I just started making my own list and shared it with him; he complained about every one of them so finally started contributing a few of his own. Then when I began encouraging him to help me reach the magic "27" he made all sorts of excuses about things he had to do and how it was wasting his time. I got him to stick it out by invoking the magic name of "Lynn Durham."

Completing the list ABSOLUTELY gave us both a sense of greater control over our lives. I then asked him to prioritize what he thought would be the FIRST most likely source of fast revenue, the second, etc, and to do that for EACH of us -- a HIS and HER list of priorities to pull us out of this hole we're in. I reminded him that between us we have TWO of the brightest, most well-educated, multi-talented, highly experienced people I know working together and that SURELY -- BETWEEN US -- we can manage to survive this little blip in the road without calling on someone else to bail us out. We would expect no less of others in our lives -- our CHILDREN for instance -- whom we either EXPECT or are trying to teach to be more self-reliant.

All I can say is it worked, and it worked way better than any words of encouragement or advice I could have given him about what to do -- which he would have probably resented or become defensive about, as he has in the past.

I'm feeling very grateful for YOU and want you to know what a powerful influence you are in my life. You help me appreciate what I have; "get a grip" on what I think I can't; and move forward when I'm stuck."

Isn't it interesting how the action of coming up with ideas changed the emotion. Her feeling of being victimized changed into feeling empowered.

I have used this same method with my son when we were having a disagreement. We started searching for 27 ideas for solutions. One of his was, "You can buy me a car." I was a single mom, money was tight and he was well aware of it. We both knew that wasn't happening. I wrote down, "I could buy you a car." That idea was something that made us both chuckle and with that laughter came a change of emotion that made the interaction go much better. At this point I can't remember what the disagreement was about or how it was solved. But I remember how the exercise softened our feelings and I do know that it brought us to a resolution of our challenge.

 HERE'S ONE THOUGHT: I'm going to go beyond Z and find at least 27 ideas!

Ideas are the currency of success. They separate you from your competition. Edward DeBono

SPILLED MILK PUZZLE

Creativity can be used in many ways. Some friends who moved out of the area used it in their gift giving. A group of friends gave them a surprise going-away party at a local restaurant. I don't recall what we purchased for them. I do, however, remember the gift they gave us, not the one they purchased to leave with us. The gift that made such a lasting impression on me was one that was creative and fun.

I don't know if you know what a "spilled milk" puzzle is. Picture spilled milk, all white with an irregular border. It is a challenging jigsaw puzzle because there are no straight lines or pictures to help with the assembly of the pieces. Suzy and Tom bought one of those puzzles, put it together and wrote clues on it for a treasure hunt. Then they proceeded to take it apart giving one section of pieces to each couple with the instructions, "Put your part of the puzzle together. Then gather the friends to reassemble it in order to read the directions."

We put our respective sections together and then planned the night for the rendezvous. All the pieces and parts were united and the hunt began using the clues we found there. I remember the hiding place ended up being in a doghouse, but I can't think of what the "treasure" was.

Their gift-giving was not about money. The important gifts our friends gave us were:

From Frazzled To Fantastic!

remembrance of them, their creativity and fun for life
reconnecting the friends they left behind, and
the *laughter and joy* we experienced that evening.

What innovative ways can you think of to bring more joy to your world?

Suzy wrote to me to tell me what I didn't remember, but I think it's almost better the way I wrote it than remembering the gifts per say.

"Yes, there were gold chocolate coins, and bottles of wine coolers! You guys had a surprise party at the restaurant. Linda and Jim were supposedly taking us out to dinner, and there were all of our friends! We had no idea you guys had planned it! You gave us an album with pictures and a letter from each of you. I still look at it once in a while. By the way, it took me DAYS to put together that white puzzle! And I was so busy doing everything else for moving. I am so glad you even remembered it. No one else has ever mentioned it."

 HERE'S ONE THOUGHT: How can I be more creative in adding joy to my world?

Your brain creates new neurons and neural connections throughout your entire life! Physical and cognitive exercise can stimulate this process increasing the number of neural connections. ... Be social: Interacting with others supports cognitive health by exercising diverse areas of the brain. www.luminosity.com

THE ARTIST WITHIN

We have all kinds of growing edges in our lives and I invite you to go to those edges and expand them. What creative interest do you feel drawn to? When you get in touch and nourish your spirit with the arts, it's healing. There are even organizations such as the Society for the Arts in Health Care that support healing with art.

I know what a natural high comes from art. I have done oils, watercolor and pen and ink drawings. How relaxed you can feel when you're doing it.

Journal, paint, craft, dance, sing, write a poem, play an instrument, tell a story, plant a garden, do woodworking, ski, sail, whatever you feel drawn to accomplish. Embrace it and celebrate life. Release your creative spirit, the healer within. Everyone is an artist.

Release your critic and welcome your inner child. Art is about creating a space and taking time for yourself, it's an invitation to do what attracts you.

Whether it's a distraction, a focused intention or the sense of controlling something when all else seems out of your control, bringing something into existence is a natural high.

Value yourself enough to do what you love. The stories of how art has healed have come from the people who have been healed by it.

Since ancient times, healers have used song and chanting. It has been shown to alleviate stress, elevate moods, help with clear thinking, reduce pain, and promote healing. YOU know what songs elevate your spirit. Are they the sounds you have in your life?

Over 2,500 years ago, Pythagoras, the Greek philosopher, advocated singing and playing a musical instrument every day to purge the body of worry, sorrow, fear and anger. How can you let the good vibrations in? And how can you let your music out?

Many of these activities include being around other people. Sometimes when you feel most unraveled, it's time to reconnect with other people. Love is the fabric of our lives.

You are worth it, it's good for you, find something you love to do.

And then do it!

 HERE'S ONE THOUGHT: I always loved to or wanted to _____ I'm making an appointment to bring it into my life.

The problem is not that there are problems. The problem is expecting otherwise and thinking that having problems is a problem. Theodore Rubin

BRAIN BLOSSOM SOLUTIONS

Worried, focused on problems? Is that your legacy?

I received a clever e-mail on how you know when you have to join *e-mail anonymous.* One of the items was: "You can't call your mother – she doesn't have a modem." One day I called my Internet service provider (ISP) because I couldn't send my messages, and one of those items was extremely important to get out. The recipient needed it that day. There was something wrong at the ISP and the trouble wouldn't be repaired for a while, not until after I had to leave my office. We talked about what we could do and the representative was kind enough to offer to write down the message and send it for me when the server was back up and running. As I started to dictate the information, I had a startling revelation, I could use the telephone!

I could call the person on the phone and give them the detailed information I was giving to the service person. What a concept! Phone them! Why had it taken so long for that thought to come to me? Now that I think of it, I could have FAXed it to them as well.

The most startling fact of the revelation was why I had only focused on e-mail, especially since it wasn't working. E-mail was what we had been using but it didn't have to be.

Many times we have a plan and forget to consider the myriad of solutions. In this instance, the person I wanted to e-mail wasn't all that far away; I could even have driven my message there.

"Brain blossom" numerous ways to meet your challenges. When you keep your eyes on a problem, it fills your field of vision, not allowing any room for the creativity to flourish. The more practice we gain in taking our focus off the problems and looking for solutions, the better we become at helping to bloom ideas.

Do you teach your children to shift their focus to solutions? The next time one of them comes to you with a problem, sit down with a pencil and paper and think of the all the ways it can be resolved. Write down every solution that comes to your mind and theirs. The more off-beat ideas just add to the joy. Relax and allow creativity to reign. Wouldn't you like to teach your kids to have fun and to be flexible with new ideas?

Sometimes the solutions are not readily visible. During those times, are you willing to wait and put the concern aside? Do you show your children how to do this? Have you ever found when you went about your business, doing what is immediately before you, some problems just solve themselves?

In other circumstances, maybe you need to place your concern in God's hands with faith. Going into the silence, even for a moment, and asking God's will for you helps you to center and make wiser decisions. What about trust in God as a lesson for your children? What a gift your children would have if you could leave that legacy.

By the way, what legacy are you leaving? How do you want to be remembered? I hope people will say, "She brought me peace, love or joy."

I haven't named my children Yahoo, AOL or dotcom. But another sign of questionable email addiction was smiling with your head tilted! That could be mine ;-). I'll smile straight, right-sided, left-sided, even upside down if I have to. For me, it doesn't matter how your head is tilted – just keep smiling and trusting. It changes your body chemistry. You're one smile away from feeling better!

And remember, if your mom doesn't have email, you can use the telephone.com ;-)

 HERE'S ONE THOUGHT: Let me rest in the solutions.

TRUSTING THE FUTURE

Life is not a journey to the grave with the intention of
arriving safely in a pretty and well preserved body; but
rather to "skid in" broadside, thoroughly used up, totally
worn out, and loudly proclaiming, "WOW! What a Ride!"
Maxine Cartoon

As you look toward the future, be careful about choosing stressful thoughts. So many things are affected all the way down to the telomeres on the DNA. Molecular biologist Elizabeth Blackburn and health psychologist Elissa Epel showed that chronic stress may actually gnaw at DNA, increasing the aging process. In their studies they showed it was the stress the people *felt*, more than the actual circumstances they were in that was responsible for the greatest damage. Thea Singer in her book *Stress Less* says, "The results replicated those of Blackburn and Epel's earlier cross-section study with the caregiver moms: Those who *perceived* themselves as being under greater stress had shorter telomeres at the study's start than those who didn't – caregivers and controls alike. What blew the scientists' socks off (OK their lab coats) was that after twelve months the telomeres actually *lengthened* in those caregivers whose stress levels had dropped. In just one short year of stressing less, their biological aging had not just slowed but had *reversed.*"

Singer describes how telomeres help save chromosomes and are a powerful cancer deterrent.

I know that many people feel "damaged." My logo is a heart with one wing because I believe we can do it on a wing and a prayer, we just need the right thought to hold onto.

Our brain can change. You can make new thoughts instead of the ones that you go to automatically. It just takes a little practice.

I know several friends who had accidents and were told they would not walk again. One man spent 15 years in a wheel chair and worked *very* hard with someone who believed he could walk. I met him dancing. He is now a dance instructor in his 70's and moving so fast and so gracefully it's amazing for anyone of any age.

So looking to the future, if you want your future to be happier and longer, watch your thinking and your feeling.

 HERE'S ONE THOUGHT: What's the best thought here to lengthen my telomeres?

The shell must be cracked apart if what is in it is to come out, for if you want the kernel, you must break the shell. Meister Eckhart

GET HATCHED

When you feel like you're ready to break, relax. You're not cracking up, just cracking open!

There are many people who have watched the hatching of eggs, at least in a science project. Since I didn't do that experiment in fifth grade, I did it just recently! You get the eggs, put them in an incubator and adjust the temperature to keep them warm maybe with a light. And twice daily you turn them while you wait.

How many of us feel like an egg with the heat turned on? How many feel that it has been a long, long wait? The light is "out there," but we're waiting in complete darkness. Maybe we feel we are getting turned around.

After all that heat and all that waiting, there is still the work to crack open the shell. Pecking, pecking and pecking just to get a small break in it. More work to crack it open, more tapping and rapping, and the aperture widens a little. More struggle ensues and then, finally, the big push to get out.

Drum roll please.

Eureka! You've arrived!

But wait...

All that's there is a weak, wobbly, wet, featherless thing. This can't be the finished product.

162

How many of us have felt that way? After all that waiting, twisting and turning, and working and pushing, we aren't there yet. (Wherever that elusive "there" is exactly, I'm not sure.)

We thought we were ready, but still there is more patience required, more growing to do, more learning is necessary, in addition to...more waiting.

On it goes, gaining strength, growing feathers, eating worms, and finally, not pushing but getting pushed. Out you go! Hopefully, it's "wheee," not "thump." Either way, it's time to get flapping.

But what's the alternative? Do nothing? We either risk it or rot. Eggs don't fly. Life invites you, just like the childhood saying, "Come out, come out, wherever you are."

And so it goes. You attempted to walk, and it worked. Even after that success, some of us are prisoners of our own choosing, unwilling to attempt, afraid to risk failure, resistant to let go of our old environment. We need to try new things.

What do you think you want to do? Will you be willing to risk? What's hatching in you?

Some things will work; some may not, but not to try, to stay still for too long, may cause you to "go bad."

 HERE'S ONE THOUGHT: Some hatch and some don't. I'm going to be the one to break out... and then....fly!

In times of crisis, meaning is strength. But the deepest meaning is carried in the unconscious mind, whose language is the language of dreams, of symbols and archetypes. Poetry speaks this language and helps us hear meaning in illness, in the events of our lives often for the first time. Finding such meaning feels like revelation. Like grace. Rachael Naomi Remen, MD

POETIC MEDICINE

In one of my programs on stress hardiness, I closed with a poem I had recently written at the time called, "Life Asked Me to Dance." A woman came up to me and said, "I've heard that poem before." That surprised me because it was so new. She went on to tell me where, and I remembered the call to ask permission to use the poem.

It was for a singles' group. They were planning a dinner dance. The interesting part of the story was about a man who was in the group. He had told several members that he would be there for dinner but he wasn't staying for the dance. He made it clear to several of the women that he was coming to eat, reminding them not to ask him to stay to dance, he was leaving.

After dinner was over, someone read the poem. He chose to stay, got up and danced, and had a wonderful time.

I've watched someone read this poem and cry. Many have come up to me after a program and asked if they could get a copy. When I was interviewed on TV, the host wished he had read the poem before the program. If he had, he would have asked me to recite it on the air because he thought it would help someone. I hear how it's moved people. It's on my audio book *Dancing Gracefully with Life* with wonderful music behind it. If you are interested in a copy of the poem email me. I'll send it to you. (smile@lynndurham.com)

This highlights the power of our words. They cannot be taken lightly. What is your intention for the words you share?

I've heard it's best to make your words tender. If you won't do it for those around you, how about doing it for yourself? It would be important just in case later you have to eat them!

 HERE'S ONE THOUGHT: No matter what others do, I choose to live my life as I wish; my words will lift others and me too!

It does not matter how slowly you go, so long as you do not stop. Confucius

PIONEERS OF AMERICA

I flew out to see my son Tyler in Montana. Looking out the plane window at the great expanse of land, I was in awe of the adventuresome spirit and strength of those pioneers who *walked* out West.

As if the mere distance wasn't daunting enough, I noticed the meandering rivers, snaking back and forth for miles. I thought about the people walking alongside the water until they could find a suitable place to cross with all their belongings. Trudging along the S curves, going so many more steps than it seemed necessary, looking for the "best" place to risk negotiating the waters.

Then the hills got bigger. What did they think when they first saw what they would have to surmount? The upward pull going for so long? And when they crossed over one, there would be another and another.

Some people broke off, decided they had gone far enough and would settle where they were. Some pushed on, crossing the Rockies to the fertile lands of California. Some turned back. Which person would you have been?

Maybe you would have been the one who stayed back East? Or might you have been the one who ventured out and then stopped along the way to establish a new life? Or would you have continued on to reach your goal with patient endurance?

166

What happened along the way? Were there family members or friends buried along the trail? Did you sing or dance? Were you hungry or was there enough to eat?

Each pioneer would have challenges to overcome, different ones depending on their choices to stay, to stop, to go on, or to go back. Did each succeed to the level of their strength?

If you were to rise up and look back over the journey you took as a traveler in this life, what would you see?

Can you notice the sticking parts, the successes, the wait-training, the parts that built your faith muscles? Did you take the circuitous route? There were probably ups and downs. Did you have an ultimate goal? Were you willing to do what was difficult to do to get there, to keep moving toward it, wading through or climbing over the things that seemed to block the way?

Each step of the journey brought new threads to be woven into the fabric of each life. Each life has its own colors and patterns, thickness and texture. And they all have their particular charm and beauty when viewed from a distance, like a tapestry, a patchwork of farms and fields, roads and river beds, mountains and plains.

I can't imagine what that journey was like for the pioneers. And I don't know what life is like for you. As for me, I don't know exactly what comes next. I just take the next step and the next, moving in the direction I have chosen.

The view was breathtakingly beautiful - the rivers, the mountains, the farm fields and the plains. Maybe that's what it's like when we look back at our lives from a higher perspective. It's extravagantly beautiful, wonder-filled!

HERE'S ONE THOUGHT: I am building my faith muscles as I pioneer and discover my own life.

Follow your bliss. Joseph Campbell

SECOND CHANCES

When my oldest son was a preschooler, he heard his grandmother say, "Oh, Brett, I'm getting old." He must have been worried about his own status because he checked in with, "But I'm still new, right?" The older I get, the more I see that we are all "still new." Creating and recreating in every moment. You have the power to change and become a "new" person.

Hopefully, you will find some "new" thoughts here. Tom wrote to me wondering if thoughts should have freshness dating labels on them! He asked, "When thoughts "get old" would they be smelly?" Maybe some could, but others may be like gold, increasing in value.

You're creating your own future, one thought at a time! How will you invest?

Are you willing to claim possession of what is rightfully your own? Ask what makes you come alive and design your decisions in alignment with your dreams. The *Butterfly Effect* is the informal name for the phenomenon of how tiny changes in input can create an overwhelmingly different output. Invest means more than committing capital to gain profit. It also means to endow with authority or power. Fashion your life so you can inaugurate yourself with ceremony into the achievement of your heart's desire. Each *second* is a choice point and you're creating your own future, invest in success.

169

Now that you have this information you have a second chance to choose the thoughts you hold. What I want people to know, there are "second" chances. Not one and two (first and second) but new chances in each of our "seconds" to choose again, to choose a new way of thinking, speaking, acting and being. And that different choice of thought, will change lives. People will feel better and move From *Frazzled to Fantastic!*

 HERE'S ONE THOUGHT: This is a new second, another "second" chance for me. I'll choose carefully what I think.

And also...

All that having been said, about changing your thoughts, I have a couple other ideas that I tested out as well.

I believe that sometimes the greater wisdom comes in acknowledging and embracing your pain.

Instead of directing pain inward causing depression, we could direct it outward in a physical activity. I have used running, chopping wood, and breaking eggs to "ex-press" as in pressing out, the pain.

Another technique is noticing where we "feel" things in our bodies, and being willing to be with that pain or sensation. I've been surprised at how that shifts things as well. Check out www.livingthequestions.com.

I've helped people with the acupressure called Emotional Freedom Technique. Little miracles occurred as they tapped and moved their eyes to feeling better, amazed at how well it worked.

And another personal story - when I was going through a divorce, I wanted to be stoic. The tears had only been welling in my eyes at times. I had not fully embraced the pain I had been feeling. So one weekend I did just that. I cried and sobbed and felt my sadness fully. I noticed that the crying came to a natural stopping point. We may think that if we start to cry we won't be able to stop, but I've never heard of anyone who could not stop crying in any medical reports!

Journaling about this experience later I found wisdom that came through my fingers to the paper. I wrote, "I embraced the pain and it disappeared in my arms and I was left holding myself. Ah, so that's what it's all about - loving me."

If we are to love others as ourselves, then I guess we better love ourselves first and with an overflowing love. Wouldn't it be great if LOVE was what ran through us, poured out of us onto people and situations around us? You can use your thoughts to focus on love for you and for others by asking, "What would love do here?"

 HERE'S ONE THOUGHT: *Love lives through, with and in me. What would Love do here?*

FINAL THOUGHTS

Since genetics is now intimately linked to mind and consciousness, the key to healing ultimately lies in controlling your beliefs and emotions. Bottom line: mind your thoughts! We've always taught our children the importance of controlling their behavior. But maybe it's time to focus more on teaching them how to control what they think and feel, since beliefs and emotions are what trigger the expression of specific DNA. Behavior will naturally follow. Even more importantly, what you think and feel may affect the DNA of your children, your grandchildren, and their children. I can't say it better than Dawson Church: "The code imprinted in our DNA, the one thing we thought was for certain, is just waiting for direction by us to change, creating a civilization that brings health, happiness, and vibrancy in ways in which the current medical establishment only dreams of. Joseph Mercola, MD

What if we can help the health of our children and grandchildren? What if the energy we send out can change the world? What you think may be more important than you ever imagined. Isn't it time you started to pay attention and choose life enhancing thoughts?

Be sure to let me know if anything here has helped you. If you have suggestions about other thoughts that worked for you, let me know that as well. I wish for you - wonderful thoughts...ones that will move you *from frazzled to fantastic!*

Blessings, Lynn

Lynn Durham

FURTHER INFORMATION

Since you may have at least flipped through this book, you are well aware it is by no means an exhaustive research project. Actually, it is not a research project at all. The most it would be is with you as the researcher, testing the ideas in your life. I did however want to include some references for further reading or study in case you have interest.

Several of these books I've chosen because of the great reference sections at the back so you can find even more information to back up what I've said. Some websites are rich with facts and some things are listed here... just because.

A few favorite authors to bring you peaceful thoughts are Rachael Naomi Remen, Wayne Dyer, Paul Pearsall, Thich Nhat Hanh, Louise Hay, Wayne Muller and Anthony DeMello.

THE GLAD GAME

-Childre, Doc Lew. *Freeze Frame*. Boulder Creek, CA; Planetary Publications; 1994.

-Emmons, R.A. and McCullough, M.E. *The Psychology of Gratitude*. New York: Oxford University Press, 2004.

-Seligman, Martin, PhD. *Learned Optimism*. New York, New York; Alfred A. Knopf, Inc. 1990. And his website on Positive Psychology: http://www.ppc.sas.upenn.edu/index.html

-www.heartmath.org/research/science-of-the-heart/heart-rate-variability.html

-www.tallycounterstore.com (for counting your blessings!)

EMBRACING WHAT IZ

-Frankl, Viktor, E. MD, PhD. *Man's Search for Meaning.* Boston, MA; Beacon Press; 1963.
-Ornish, Dean, MD. *Reversing Heart Disease.* New York, New York; Ballantine Books; 1996.
-Selye, Hans, M.D. *Stress without Distress.* New York, New York; Lippincott and Crowell, Publishers; 1974. The doctor who originally noted the connection between stress and disease.
-www.thework.org For the *Judge-Your-Neighbor* Worksheet and it also has great video clips of Katie doing "the work."

SERVING WITH LOVE

-Lawson, Douglas M. PhD. *Give to Live, How Giving Can Change Your Life.* LaJolla, CA; ALTI Publishing; 1991.
-www.unlimitedloveinstitute.org/ For information about altruism, service and compassion.

CHERISHING EACH OTHER

-Ornish, Dean, MD. *Love and Survival.* New York, New York: HarperCollins Publishers, Inc; 1998.
-Selhub, Eva M, MD. *The Love Response.* New York: Ballentine Books, 2009.
-Worthington, Everett, L. Jr. Editor. *Dimensions of Forgiveness - Psychological Research and Theological Perspectives.* Philadelphia; Templeton Foundation Press; 1998.

LIVING IN THE PLEASANT

-Berk, Lee S. MPH, Dr.PH, Felten, David L. MD, PhD, Tan, Stanley A. MD, PhD, et al. "Modulation of Neuroimmune Parameters During the Eustress of Humor-Associated Mirthful Laughter," *Alternative Therapies in Health and Medicine*, March 2000, Vol. 7, No. 2, 62-75.

-Dossey, Larry, MD. "Now You Are Fit To Live: Humor and Health." *Alternative Therapies*; Sept, 1996. Vol.2 No. 5. 55-63.
-www.aath.org/humor_resources.htm Association for Applied and Therapeutic Humor

LETTING GO
-www.peacepilgrim.com
-www.yesfactor.com

GET CREATIVE JUICES FLOWING
-Fox, John. *Poetic Medicine.* New York, New York: Jeremy P. Tarcher/Putnam; 1997.
-Rollin McCraty, Ph.D., Mike Atkinson, Glen Rein, Ph.D. and Alan D. Watkins, MBBS. "Music Enhances the Effect of Positive Emotional States on Salivary IGA," *Stress Medicine.* 1996; 12 (3): 167-175
-www.cdss.org/ Country Dance and Song Society
-www.edwdebono.com/ On creativity
-www.mozarteffect.com/
-www.thesah.org The Society for the Arts in Health Care

TRUSTING THE FUTURE
-Amen, Daniel G. *Change Your Brian, Change Your Life.* New York, New York: Three Rivers Press. 1998.
-Doidge, Norman, MD. *The Brain That Changes Itself: Stories of Person Triumph from the Frontiers of Brain Science.* New York, New York, 2007.
-Lipton, Bruce PhD. *The Biology of Belief: Unleashing the Power of Consciousness, Matter and Miracles,* Hay House, 2011.
-Singer, Thea. *Stress Less: The New Science That Shows Women How to Rejuvenate the Body and the Mind.* New York, New York; Hudson Street Press, 2010.

QUESTIONS

If you have a book club and would like to schedule a phone conference or personal visit, please contact me at 603-926-9700 or smile@LynnDurham.com.

Here are some ideas for book club discussion or individual journaling:

1. Did you test changing your thoughts from things that annoy you to things you appreciate? How did it work for you?

2. Have you noticed that you are resisting things, people or situations in your life? Have you ever tried to embrace what is? What did you notice?

3. Do you listen to your inner voice? Can you hear one? What have you heard in the past? Have you acted on it?

4. When you are helping someone else how does it feel? Does it take your focus off your own problems? Have you served and not wanted to? What's the difference?

5. Can you think of a time when a child gave *you* wisdom? How important for your children is what you model for them?

6. Is there a "trigger point therapist" in your life? Have you ever felt the difference that forgiveness makes?

7. Tell or write a story that made you laugh. What experience did you have that didn't seem so funny when it happened but has gained in humor with time?

8. What in your life would be better if you were willing to release it with love? Do you feel that you have to be perfect?
9. Is there an activity that you used to do and enjoy that you could bring back into your life? How do you feel when you're creating?
10. What is it that you would like to do? What would you do if you knew that you would be successful?
11. What thought presented here was the most significant to you?
12. Are you committing to do something different for yourself in the future?

ABOUT THE AUTHOR

A registered nurse and mother of three sons, Lynn Durham focuses on wellness. She has been, or presently is, an adjunct professor, columnist, speaker, consultant, retreat leader and personal well-being coach. Lynn blends the knowledge of a professor of nursing education, the wisdom gained at the Harvard Deaconess Mind Body Medical Institute and mixes it with life experiences, optimism and obvious joy.

Through her writing, speaking, TV or radio appearances, individuals at companies, associations, and schools are changing the way they see their world. Lynn has been called "a creative antidote to the challenges of day to day business ...and... life." After connecting with Lynn and her light-hearted approach people never see things quite the same again and feel better for it.

Lynn grew up along the Connecticut shore, raised her boys in the New Hampshire seacoast area and now lives near the mountains and lakes. She writes from her story filled eighteenth century home located near "Golden Pond," the same house where it's said Kate Douglas Wiggin wrote *Rebecca of Sunnybrook Farm* as a guest when it was open to tourists.

Also by Lynn: the audio book *Dancing Gracefully with Life*, and the booklet *Welcome Wellness*. She is contributing author to several books including *Touched By Angels of Mercy* a book about caregivers.

For more information about Lynn's speaking, writing, or programs please email smile@LynnDurham.com, call 603-926-9700, or sign up for a newsletter on her website: www.LynnDurham.com.

Made in the USA
Middletown, DE
02 June 2017